THE BIG BUG BOOK

This edition is published by Hermes House

Hermes House is an imprint of Anness Publishing Ltd
Hermes House, 88–89 Blackfriars Road, London SE1 8HA
tel. 020 7401 2077; fax 020 7633 9499
www.lorenzbooks.com; info@anness.com

© Anness Publishing Ltd 2002, 2005

A CIP catalogue record for this book is available from the British Library.

Publisher: Joanna Lorenz
Managing Editor: Linda Fraser
Compendium Editor: Joy Wotton
Authors: Barbara Taylor (*Introducing Bugs and Minibeasts*),
Dr Jen Green (*Spiders, Beetles and Bugs* and *Social Insects*)
and John Farndon (*Butterflies and Moths*)
Consultants: Dr Sarah A. Corbett (*Spiders* and *Social Insects*), Mathew Frith
(*Beetles and Bugs*) and Michael Chinery (*Butterflies and Moths*)
Designers: Traffika Publishing Ltd, Mirjana Nociar, Jill Mumford, Vivienne Gordon, Sarah Williams
Illustrators: Julian Baker, Vanessa Card, Stuart Carter, Rob Sheffield, David Webb
Production Controller: Steve Lang

Previously published in four separate volumes,
Spiders, Beetles and Bugs, Butterflies and Moths and *Insect Societies*

1 3 5 7 9 10 8 6 4 2

THE BIG BUG BOOK

DISCOVER THE AMAZING WORLD OF BEETLES, BUGS, BUTTERFLIES, MOTHS, INSECTS AND SPIDERS

BARBARA TAYLOR
DR JEN GREEN
JOHN FARNDON

HERMES HOUSE

CONTENTS

Introducing Bugs and Minibeasts 6

Introducing Bugs and Minibeasts

Did you know that three-quarters of all animals are insects – and that one in every five animals on Earth is a beetle? Here is a detailed look at the world's most numerous and successful creatures, the insects, together with their relatives, the hairy hunters called spiders. There are 35,000 known species (kinds) of spider, which sounds a huge number until you compare this with the more than one million different species of insect, including more than 350,000 beetles and about 145,000 moths.

Among the fascinating insects and spiders you will find in this book are fireflies that glow in the dark, silk worms that spin beautiful thread, monarch butterflies that migrate over 3000 kilometres and spiders that live underwater in silken diving bells.

There are more than 4,000 different types of ladybirds in temperate and tropical countries all over the world.

Small insects and minibeasts

Almost all insects and spiders are small. There are butterflies that are smaller than a postage stamp and the smallest spider is as tiny as a full stop. Most of the biggest insects and spiders would fit on a person's hand. Such animals are often called minibeasts, as are similar creatures such as woodlice, scorpions and centipedes.

Features that insects and spiders have in common include the lack of a backbone (they are invertebrates), their tough outer shell, or exoskeleton, and the fact they are cold-blooded, which means their bodies are a similar temperature to their surroundings. Most insects and spiders live on their own, but a few (such as ants, bees and wasps) are social and live and work together in groups called colonies.

head

thorax

abdomen

Insects don't have a backbone, instead they have a tough outer shell. They have three main body parts: the head, the thorax and the abdomen.

Different bodies

Insects and spiders are different in many ways. Insects have three body parts and six legs, whereas spiders have only two body parts and eight legs. Most insects have wings and antennae. Spiders have neither, so they cannot fly.

Spiders are all carnivores (meat-eaters), and nearly all spiders use poison (venom) to kill or paralyse their prey, or for defence. Insect diets are more varied and only some insects are poisonous. Some insects are herbivores (plant-eaters), some are carnivores and larvae (young insects) often eat different foods from their parents.

abdomen

cephalothorax

Spiders have two basic body parts: the abdomen and the cephalothorax. They are unlike insects since they have eight legs rather than six.

On the wing

Bees, butterflies, beetles, bugs and other insects are the only animals without backbones that are able to fly. They were the first creatures on Earth to fly, more than 350 million years ago.

Most insects fly by beating their wings very rapidly. Butterflies and moths fly in a similar way to birds by rippling their wings slowly up and down and gliding on currents of air. They can fly huge distances across land and sea without running out of energy.

The appearance of the wings is often characteristic of different insect groups. Butterflies and moths have scaly wings, while other insects, such as bees, wasps, beetles, bugs and flies, have transparent (see-through) wings. In beetles, the front pair of wings have become hard wing cases, which protect the delicate flying wings underneath. Some bugs have hard bases to their front wings. Flies have only one pair of wings and most ants and termites have no wings at all.

Butterflies fly in a similar way to birds by rippling their wings slowly up and down. The wings push air backwards to drive the butterfly forward in the air. As the wings come down, they provide lift, which helps keep the butterfly up in the air.

Life cycles

All spiders and almost all insects hatch from eggs. Baby spiders look like tiny adults when they hatch out of their eggs, so they have a two-stage life cycle. Bugs, termites, dragonflies and grasshoppers have three stages to their life cycle. The egg hatches into a nymph, which grows and moults (sheds its skin) several times before becoming an adult.

Butterflies, moths, beetles, bees, wasps and ants have a four-stage life cycle – egg, larva (grub or caterpillar), pupa and adult. The caterpillar is the feeding stage, and a caterpillar can eat its way through several times its own body weight in food each day. The pupa is the resting stage. Inside the pupa, the larva's body is broken down into a chemical soup and then rebuilt into an adult's body. This astonishing process of transformation is called complete metamorphosis.

The three-stage life cycle of bugs, dragonflies, termites and grasshoppers is called incomplete metamorphosis because there is no pupal stage and it does not involve totally rebuilding the body.

As soon as a caterpillar bites its way out of an egg it begins eating. This Privet Hawk moth caterpillar is in the second stage of its life cycle. It will become an adult after it has gone through the pupa stage.

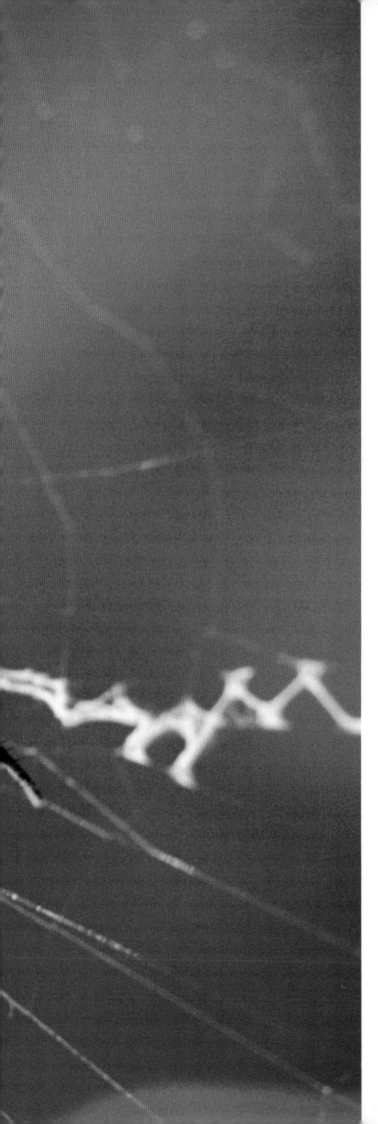

SPIDERS

Terrifying tarantulas, deadly black widows, huge, hairy spiders trapped in the bath … is this how you think of spiders? You may be surprised to learn that only about 30 kinds of spider are dangerous to people and that most tarantulas are shy, timid creatures with a bite no more painful than a wasp sting. The real lives of spiders are much more amazing than scary. Spiders produce silk that is stronger than steel and stickier than sticky tape. Jumping spiders stalk their prey like tigers while spitting spiders glue their prey to the ground. There are even spiders that look like crabs, ants or wasps!

Introducing Spiders

Spiders are some of the most feared and least understood creatures in the animal world. These hairy hunters are famous for spinning silk and giving a poisonous bite. There are around 35,000 known species (kinds) of spider, with probably another 35,000 waiting to be discovered. Only about 30 species, however, are dangerous to people. Spiders are very useful to humans, because they eat insect pests and keep their numbers down. Spiders live nearly everywhere, from forests, deserts and grasslands, to caves, ships and in our homes. Some spin webs to catch their prey while others leap out from a hiding place or stalk their meals like tigers. There are even spiders that fish for their supper and one that lives in an air bubble underwater.

The front part of a spider is a joined head and chest called the cephalothorax. The body is covered by a hard skin called an exoskeleton. The shield-like plate on the top of the cephalothorax is called the carapace.

Spiders use palps for holding food and as feelers.

The chelicerae (jaws) are used to bite and crush prey. Each ends in a fang that injects poison.

A spider's eight hollow legs are joined to the cephalothorax.

The abdomen is the rear part of a spider. It is covered by soft, stretchy skin.

Silk is spun by organs called spinnerets at the back of the abdomen.

◄ **WHAT IS A SPIDER?**
Spiders are often confused with insects, but they belong to a completely different group. A spider has eight legs, but an insect has six. Its body has two parts while an insect's has three. Many insects have wings and antennae, but spiders do not.

WEB WEAVERS ▶

About half of all spiders spin webs. They know how to do this by instinct from birth, without being taught. Many spiders build a new web each night. They build webs to catch prey. Spiders have a good sense of touch and can quickly tell if anything is caught in the web.

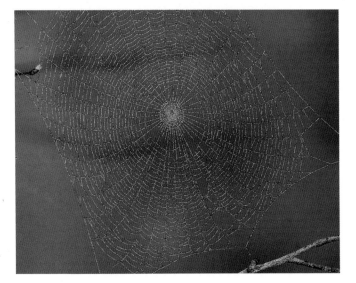

— Bright colours help to conceal this spider among flowers.

▲ **SPIDER SHAPES AND COLOURS**

The triangular spider (*Arcys*) is named after its brightly coloured abdomen, which is shaped like a triangle. Its colour and shape help it to hide in wait for prey on leaves and flowers. Other spiders use bright colours to warn their enemies that they taste nasty.

Arachne's Tale
A Greek legend tells of Arachne, a girl who was very skilled at weaving. The goddess Athene challenged her to a contest, which Arachne won. The goddess became so cross Arachne killed herself. Athene was sorry and turned the girl into a spider so she could spin forever. The Latin name for spiders is arachnids, named after Arachne.

◀ **MALES AND FEMALES**

Female spiders are usually bigger than the males and not so colourful, though this female *Nephila* spider is boldly marked. The male at the top of the picture is only one fifth of her size.

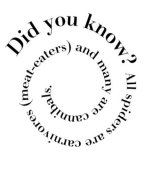

Did you know? All spiders are carnivores (meat-eaters) and many are cannibals.

Shapes and Sizes

Can you believe that there are spiders as big as frisbees or dinner plates? The world's biggest spider, the goliath tarantula of South America, is this big. Yet the smallest spider is only the size of a full stop. Apart from size, spiders also vary a great deal in their appearance. Many are an inconspicuous dull brown or grey while others are striking yellows, reds and oranges. Some spiders have short, wide bodies, while others are long, thin and skinny. There are round spiders, flat spiders and spiders with spines, warts and horns. A few spiders even look like ants, wasps or bird droppings!

▲ FLOWER SPIDERS

Using its shape and colour to hide on a flower, the flower spider (*Misumena vatia*) waits to ambush a visiting insect. This spider is one of a large family of crab spiders, so named because most of them have a similar shape to crabs.

Red-legged widow (*Latrodectus bishopi*)

Widow spiders often have bold black and red colouring.

Round, shiny abdomen.

Bristles on the back legs give the name comb-footed spider.

▲ SPINY SPIDERS

Some spiders have flat abdomens with sharp spines sticking out. This kite spider (*Gasteracantha*) has spines that look like horns. No one knows what these strange spines are for, but they may make it difficult for predators to hold or swallow the spider.

▲ GRAPE SPIDERS

Several kinds of widow spiders live in areas where grapes are grown. The females tend to have round abdomens, like a grape. Some of the most poisonous spiders belong to this group.

BIG, HAIRY SPIDERS ▶

The biggest, hairiest and scariest-looking spiders are tarantulas, or bird-eating spiders. All spiders are hairy, but tarantulas are a great deal hairier than most. Tarantulas and their relatives are called mygalomorphs and are relatively primitive spiders.

Mexican red-knee tarantula (*Brachypelma smithi*)

The red-knee tarantula is named after the orange or red markings on its legs.

Australian wolf spider (*Lycosa*)

Two large front eyes give good vision.

▲ WOLF SPIDERS

A skilled daytime hunter, this wolf spider (*Lycosa*) is brown or grey in colour. The dull colours help to hide the spider as it hunts along the ground. It has long back legs to chase after its prey.

Nephila spiders often have strikingly marked abdomens.

This female *Nephila* is much larger than the male.

Giant orb-weaver (*Nephila maculata*)

SPIDER SIZES

Spiders come in a huge range of sizes. Most spiders are tiny, with bodies less than 20mm long. The goliath tarantula, the largest spider, is 90mm long. *Patu digua*, the smallest, is just 0.37mm.

▲ GIANT WEAVERS

Some of the largest orb-web spiders in the world are species of *Nephila*. They have long cigar-shaped bodies.

Giant salmon pink bird-eater (*Lassiodora parahybana*)

Focus on

The biggest, hairiest spiders are often called tarantulas, or bird-eating spiders. The large spiders we call tarantulas are all members of the family Theraphosidae. (The true tarantula, however, is a big wolf spider from southern Europe.) There are about 800 different species of tarantula living in warm or hot places all over the world. Many live in burrows, while some are tree-dwellers. Although they look scary, most tarantulas are shy, timid creatures and are harmless to people. A few can give a very painful bite, but their poison is not deadly to humans.

WHICH NAME?

Known as tarantulas or bird-eating spiders in America and Europe, they are called baboon spiders in Africa. In Central America they are sometimes called horse spiders — their bite was falsely believed to make a horse's hoof fall off.

LIFE CYCLES

This red-knee tarantula (*Brachypelma smithi*) is shown guarding her eggs. Female tarantulas can live for more than 20 years and lay eggs at regular intervals when they become adults. After mating they may wait several months before laying their eggs.

Violet-black tarantula (*Pamphobeteus*)

Velvety, black carapace.

FLOOR WALKERS

Violet-black tarantulas live on the floor of the Amazon rainforest. These spiders are active, impressive hunters. They do not build webs or burrows, but live out in the open.

Abdomen covered in long brown hairs.

Tarantulas

TARANTULA BODIES

Essentially a tarantula's body has the same parts and works in the same way as other spiders. Its eyesight is poor and it detects prey and danger with the many sensitive hairs that cover its body. Unlike other spiders, a tarantula can flick prickly hairs off its abdomen if it is attacked. On the ends of its legs are brushes of hairs that help it to climb on smooth surfaces. These hairs let some tarantulas walk on water.

Tiger rump doppelganger (*Cyclosternum fasciata*)

The back pair of legs is used to flick hairs off the abdomen at an enemy.

Many tarantulas use their strong legs to dig out burrows.

Tarantulas have eight tiny eyes, closely grouped together.

FEARSOME FANGS

Tarantulas have large, hollow fangs that pump out venom as the spider bites. Most spiders bite with a sideways, pinching movement. Tarantulas bite straight down with great force, like a pickaxe.

FEEDING TIME

Tarantulas usually feed on insects. This *Avicularia metallica* is eating a katydid, an insect like a grasshopper. Large tarantulas are able to take much larger prey, such as birds and snakes. They are slow eaters and may drag prey back to their burrows to feed.

Arizonan blond tarantula (*Aphonopelma chalcodes*)

How Spiders Work

From the outside, a spider's body is very different from ours. It has a hard outer skeleton, called an exoskeleton, and legs that have many joints. It has eyes and a mouth, but no ears, nose or tongue. Instead, it relies on a variety of hairs and bristles to touch, taste and hear things and it smells things with microscopic pores on its feet. Inside, a spider has many features common to other animals, such as blood, nerves, a brain and a digestive system. It also has special glands for spinning silk and for making and storing poison.

▲ SPIDER SKIN
A spider's exoskeleton protects its body like a suit of armour. It is made of a stiff material called chitin. A waxy layer helps to make it waterproof. The exoskeleton cannot stretch as the spider grows so must be shed from time to time. The old skin of a huntsman spider (*Isopeda*) is shown here.

Male spiders use taste hairs to pick up scent trails left by females.

◄ HAIRY SIGNALS
The sensitive hairs covering a spider send signals to the brain alerting it to food and enemies. Tasting hairs are spread all over the spider's body. On the palps and legs, special hairs (called trichobothria) set in cup-like sockets pick up movements in the air.

▲ LEG SENSES
A green orb-weaver (*Araniella cucurbitina*) pounces on a fly. Spiders use special slits on their bodies to detect when an insect is trapped in their webs. These slits (called lyriform organs) pick up vibrations caused by a struggling insect. Nerve endings in the slits send signals to the spider's brain.

SPIDER POISON ▶

A spider is a delicate creature compared to the prey it catches. By using poison, a spider can kill its prey before the prey has a chance to harm its attacker. Spiders have two poison sacs, one for each fang. Bands of muscle around the sacs squeeze the poison down tubes in the fangs and out of a small opening in the end.

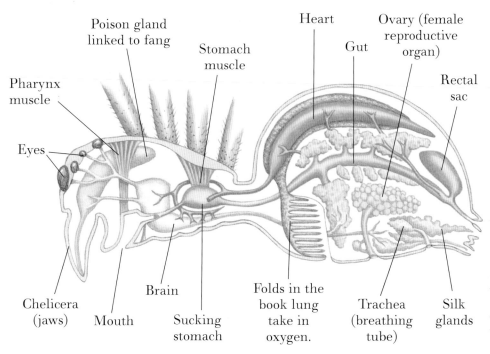

Poison gland linked to fang

Pharynx muscle

Stomach muscle

Heart

Ovary (female reproductive organ)

Rectal sac

Eyes

Chelicera (jaws)

Mouth

Brain

Sucking stomach

Folds in the book lung take in oxygen.

Trachea (breathing tube)

Silk glands

Gut

◀ **INSIDE A SPIDER**

The front part of a spider, the cephalothorax, contains the brain, poison glands, stomach and muscles. The abdomen contains the heart, lungs, breathing tubes, gut, waste disposal system, silk glands and reproductive organs. A spider's stomach works like a pump, stretching wide to pull in food that has been mashed to a soupy pulp. The heart pumps blue blood around the body.

Raiko and the Earth Spider
People have regarded spiders as dangerous, magical animals for thousands of years. This Japanese print from the 1830s shows the legendary warrior Yorimitsu (also known as Raiko) and his followers slaying the fearsome Earth Spider.

On the Move

Have you ever seen a spider scuttle swiftly away?
Spiders sometimes move quickly, but cannot keep
going for long. Their breathing system is not very
efficient so they soon run out of puff.

Spiders can walk, run, jump, climb and hang
upside down. Each spider's leg has seven sections.
The legs are powered by sets of muscles and blood
pressure. At the end of each leg are two or
three sharp claws for gripping surfaces.

Spiders that spin webs have a special claw to help
them hold on to their webs. Hunting spiders have
dense tufts of hair between the claws for gripping
smooth surfaces and for holding prey.

▲ AERONAUT
Many young or
small spiders drift
through the air on
strands of silk. Spiders
carried away on warm air
currents use this method
to find new places to live.

▲ WATER WALKER
The fishing spider (*Dolmedes fimbriatus*) is also called the raft or
swamp spider. It floats on the surface skin of water. Its long legs
spread its weight over the surface so it does not sink. Little dips
form in the stretchy skin of the water around each leg tip.

▲ SAFETY LINE
This garden spider (*Araneus*)
is climbing up a silk dragline.
Spiders drop down these lines
if they are disturbed. They
pay out the line as they go,
moving very quickly. As they
fall, spiders pull in their legs,
making them harder to see.

▲ SPIDER LEGS

Muscles in the legs of this trapdoor spider (*Aname*) bend the joints rather like we bend our knees. To stretch out the legs, however, the spider has to pump blood into them. If a spider is hurt and blood leaks out, it cannot escape from enemies.

▲ CHAMPION JUMPERS

Jumping spiders are champions of the long jump. They secure themselves with a safety line before they leap. Some species can leap more than 40 times the length of their own bodies.

▽ CLAWED FEET

Two toothed claws on the ends of a spider's feet enable it to grip surfaces as it walks. Web-building spiders have a third, middle claw that hooks over the silk lines of the web and holds the silk against barbed hairs. This allows the spider to grip the smooth, dry silk of its web without falling or slipping.

Scopulate pad

Toothed claw

Middle hook

Barbed hair

▲ HAIRY FEET

Many hunting spiders have dense tufts of short hairs called scopulae between the claws. The end of each hair is split into many tiny hairs a bit like a brush. These hairs pull up some of the moisture coating most surfaces, gluing the spider's leg down. Spiders with these feet can climb up smooth surfaces such as glass.

19

Spider Eyes

Spiders have poor eyesight and rely mainly on scents and vibrations to give them information about their surroundings. Even spiders with good eyesight, such as the jumping spiders, can see only up to 30cm away. Most spiders have eight eyes arranged in two or three rows. The eyes are pearly or dark and are usually protected by several bristles. Spider eyes are called ocelli and are of two types. Main eyes produce a focused image and help in pouncing on prey. Secondary eyes have light sensitive cells to pick up movement from a distance.

▲ NO EYES

This cave spider (*Spelungula cavernicola*) has no need for eyes, because there is no light in the cave for the spider to see. Like many animals that live in the dark it relies on other senses. It especially uses many sensitive hairs to find its way around, catch its prey and avoid enemies.

◄ BIG EYES

A spider's main eyes are always the middle pair of eyes in the front row. In most spiders the main eyes are small, but this jumping spider has very well developed main eyes, as this enlarged picture shows. They work rather like a telephoto lens on a camera. Inside, the large lens focuses light on to four layers of sensitive cells. The main eyes see clearly over a small area a few centimetres away and let the spider stalk and pounce when it gets close to its prey.

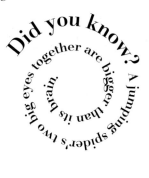

Did you know? A jumping spider's two big eyes together are bigger than its brain.

Eyes arranged
in a compact
group.

▲ HUNTSMAN SPIDER

The giant huntsman (*Holconia immanis*) is an
agile, night-time hunter. Most hunting spiders
have fairly large front eyes to help them find
and pounce on prey. Secondary eyes help the
hunters see in three dimensions over a wider
area. They detect changes in light and dark.

▲ SHORT SIGHT

Spiders that spend much of their
time under stones or in burrows usually have
small eyes. This trapdoor spider (*Aname*) has
eight tiny eyes in a close group. Spiders that
catch their prey in webs also have very poor
eyesight. These spiders rely much more on
their sense of touch than their eyesight. They
use their legs to test objects around them.

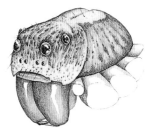

A large-eyed wolf spider
(family Lycosidae).

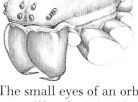

The small eyes of an orb-
weaver (family Araneidae).

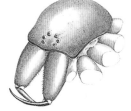

A six-eyed woodlouse
spider (family Dysderidae).

A jumping spider
(family Salticidae).

▲ EYES FOR HUNTING

The spiders with the best eyesight are active
daylight hunters such as this jumping spider.
A jumping spider's eight eyes are usually
arranged in three rows with four in the front,
two in the middle and two at the back. Lynx
spiders and wolf spiders also have good eyesight.

▲ ALL KINDS OF EYES

The position and arrangement of a spider's
eyes can be useful in telling which family it
belongs to and how it catches food. A small
number of spiders only have six eyes or fewer.
Many male money spiders have eyes on top of
little lobes or turrets sticking up from the head.

Spinning Silk

All spiders make silk. They pull the silk out of spinnerets on their abdomens, usually with their legs. The silk is a syrupy liquid when it first comes out, but pulling makes it harden. The more silk is pulled, the stronger it becomes. Some spider silk is stronger than steel wire of the same thickness. As well as being very strong, silk is incredibly thin, has more stretch than rubber and is stickier than sticky tape. Spiders make up to six different types of silk in different glands in the abdomen. Each type of silk is used for a different purpose, from making webs to wrapping prey. Female spiders produce a special silk to wrap up eggs.

An *Agroeca* spider hangs its cocoon from a grass stem. It will plaster the cocoon with mud to form a hard protective coating.

▲ EGG PARCELS

Female spiders have an extra silk gland for making egg cases called cocoons. These protect the developing eggs.

The Industrious Spider

Spiders have been admired for their tireless spinning for centuries. This picture was painted by the Italian artist Veronese in the 1500s. He wanted to depict the virtues of the great city of Venice, whose wealth was based on trade. To represent hard work and industry he painted this figure of a woman holding up a spider in its web.

▲ A SILKEN RETREAT

Many spiders build silk shelters or nests. The tube-web spider (*Segestria florentina*) occupies a hole in the bark of a tree. Its tube-shaped retreat has a number of trip lines radiating out like the spokes of a wheel. If an insect trips over a line, the spider rushes out to grab a meal.

▲ STICKY SILK

Silk oozes out through a spider's spinnerets. Two or more kinds of silk can be spun at the same time. Orb-web spiders produce gummy silk to make their webs sticky.

▲ FOOD PARCEL

A garden spider (*Araneus*) stops a grasshopper from escaping by wrapping it in silk. The prey is also paralysed by the spider's poisonous bite. Most spiders make silk for wrapping prey.

SPINNERETS ▶

A spider's spinnerets have many fine tubes on the end. The smaller tubes, or spools, produce finer silk for wrapping prey. Larger tubes, called spigots, produce coarser strands for webs.

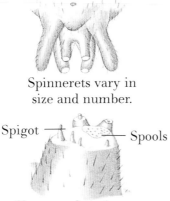

Spinnerets vary in size and number.

Spigot — Spools

Close up of a spinneret.

▲ COMBING OUT SILK

This lace-weaver (*Amaurobius*) is using its back legs to comb out a special silk. It has an extra spinning organ (the cribellum) in front of its spinnerets that produces loops of very fine silk.

▲ VELCRO SILK

The lacy webs made by cribellate spiders contain tiny loops, like velcro, that catch on the hairs and bristles of insect prey. Combined in bands with normal silk, the fluffy-looking cribellate silk stops insect prey from escaping.

Focus on

The orb-shaped (circular) web of an average garden spider (*Araneus*) is about 25cm across and uses 20 to 60m of silk. To build its web, the spider first attaches a line across a gap to form a bridge-line. The whole web will hang from this line. Suspended from the line, the spider makes a Y-shaped frame. From the hub (centre) of the Y, the spider spins a series of spoke-like threads. The spider then returns to the hub to spin a circular strengthening zone. From this zone, a temporary dry spiral of threads is laid out towards the edge of the web to hold the spokes in place. Starting from the outside, the spider now uses sticky silk to lay the final spiral. When the web is finished, the spider settles down to wait for a meal.

STICKY BEADS

As a spider spins the sticky spiral of its orb web it pulls the gummy coating into a series of beads, like a necklace. The dry spiral of silk is eaten as it is replaced. This spiral is no longer needed and the spider can recycle the nutrients it contains.

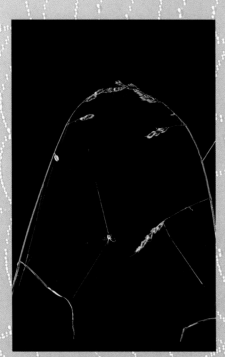

1 This garden spider is starting to spin a web. It has made a bridge-line from which it hangs down to pull the thread into a Y shape. The middle of the Y will be the centre of the web.

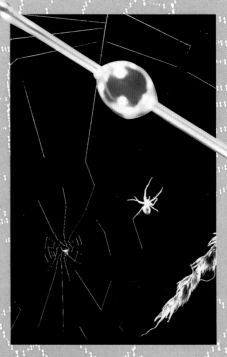

2 The spider then makes a framework, which looks like the spokes of a bicycle wheel. The spokes are called radii. From the centre, the spider now spins a dry spiral to hold the radii in place.

Spinning a Web

Spinning an orb web takes less than an hour. The spider either settles head downwards on the hub of the web, or hides in a retreat and keeps in touch through a signal thread held by the front legs.

3 Starting from the outside, the spider spins a sticky spiral. It does not go round in the same direction, but turns several times. A free zone between the sticky and dry spirals is left at the centre.

4 The completed web traps prey for long enough to give the spider time to work out its position. It feels how stretched the threads are in different parts of its web, then zooms in for the kill.

Orb-Web Spiders

The typical wheel-shaped orb web is spun by about 3,000 species of spider mostly in the family Araneidae. Some members of the Uloboridae also spin orb-shaped webs, using fluffy cribellar silk. Every orb-web spider will spin about 100 webs in its lifetime and has large silk glands. The orb web is a very clever way of trapping flying prey using the least amount of silk possible. This is important because spiders use up a lot of valuable body-building protein to spin silk. An orb web is almost invisible, yet it is very strong and elastic.

Australian orb-weaver (*Araneus*)

▲ **ORB WEAVER**
Like most orb-web spiders, this spider's abdomen is taken up by large silk glands. One gland makes the gummy silk to make its web sticky.

▲ **WEBS IN THE DEW**
Sticky beads on an orb web make it shimmer in the morning dew. The spiral threads of sticky capture silk stop flying or jumping insects from escaping.

◀ **SPINNING THE WEB**
An orb-web spider may spin a new web every night as fresh webs are the most efficient traps. The silk from old webs is usually eaten. The size of the web depends on the size of the spider — young spiders and smaller species spin smaller webs.

DECORATED WEBS ▶

Some orb weavers decorate their webs with stabilimenta (zigzags of silk). Young spiders tend to spin disc shapes, while adults build long lines.

No one is sure what they are for — some may be camouflage, but others are very obvious and may warn birds not to fly into the web.

▲ WAITING FOR A MEAL

As soon as a spider feels the vibrations made by prey struggling to escape, it moves in for the kill. It keeps its body clear of the sticky spirals, moving along the dry lines.

Did you know? One teaspoon of silk would be enough to make a million webs.

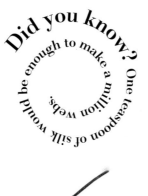

Madagascan orb-weaver (*Nephila inaurata*)

◀ GIANT NETS

Large, tropical *Nephila* spiders use tough yellow silk to build huge orb webs, some up to 2m across. These giant nets are incredibly strong and can catch small birds as prey.

The Spider and the King

In 1306, the king of Scotland Robert the Bruce was resting in a barn after defeat by the English. He watched a spider trying to spin its web. Six times the spider failed, but on the seventh attempt it succeeded. Inspired by this to fight on, Robert the Bruce finally defeated the English at Bannockburn in 1314.

Hammocks, Sheets and Scaffolds

Spiders build webs in many shapes and sizes apart from a typical orb web. Webs that look like sheets or hammocks are not sticky, but rely on a maze of criss-crossing threads to trap the prey. These are more suitable for trapping insects that walk or hop rather than those that fly. Most sheet-web spiders keep adding to their webs long after they are built. Scaffold webs have many dry, tangled threads, too, but they also have threads coated with sticky gum. Social spiders build huge communal webs that the spiders may hunt over in packs or alone.

▲ **HAMMOCK WEB**

A typical hammock web is supported by a maze of threads above and below the web. The silk is not sticky, but prey is tripped up by the threads to fall into the hammock below. The spider hangs upside down on the underside of the hammock waiting to grab prey from below and drag it through the web.

Did you know? One communal spider's web can contain up to 20,000 spiders.

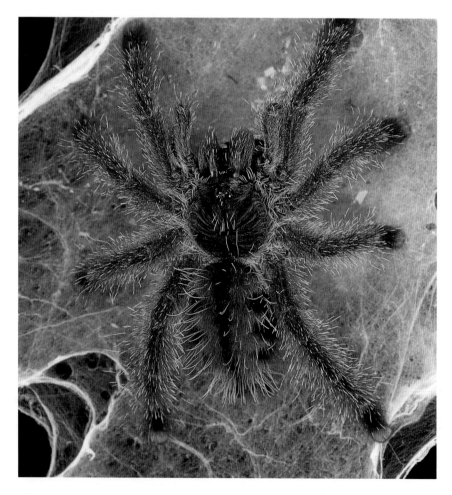

◀ **TARANTULA WEB**

Large sheet webs are made by many tarantulas, trapdoor spiders and funnel-web spiders. This pink-toed tarantula (*Avicularia avicularia*) is sitting over the entrance of its tubular web. It mostly catches tree frogs and insects.

LADEN WITH DEW ▶

The hammock webs of money spiders (family Linyphiidae) show up well in the early morning dew. These webs are so named because the central sheet of the web sags like a hammock when it is laden with dew. Most hammock webs are only a few centimetres across, but some can be as big as dinner plates. There may be 50 or more hammock webs on just one gorse bush.

▲ SPIDER CITIES

Hundreds of dome-weavers (*Cyrtophora citricola*) build their webs together in what looks like a spider city. These huge webs almost cover trees. In the centre is a domed sheet like a trampoline. Although the spiders live closely together, each one defends its own web and may attack neighbours that come too close. Young spiders build their webs inside the framework of their mother's web.

SHEET WEB ▶

The grass funnel-weaver (*Agelena labyrinthica*) builds a horizontal sheet web with a funnel-shaped shelter in one corner. The spider sits at the entrance to the funnel with its feet on the sheet waiting for an insect to get tangled in the maze of silk threads. The cobwebs made by house spiders (*Tegenaria*) in the corners of rooms are like this.

◀ SCAFFOLD WEB

Comb-footed spiders (family Theridiidae) build three-dimensional trellises called scaffold webs. This scaffold is slung over a tall plant, but there are many different kinds. Many have a thimble-shaped retreat in which the spider eats its meal. Some threads are sticky, making it difficult for insects to escape.

Sticky Traps

A few spiders do not just build a web and wait for a meal to arrive. They go fishing for their food instead. The net-casting, or ogre-faced, spider throws a strong, stretchy net over its prey. It is also named the gladiator spider after the gladiators of ancient Rome. The bolas, or angling, spider is a very unusual orb-web spider that does not spin a web. It traps insects by swinging a thin line of silk with a sticky globule on the end, like a fishing hook on the end of a line. Spitting spiders are even more cunning. They fire poisonous glue to pin their prey to the ground.

Spider-Man

The bite of a radioactive spider gave the comic book character Spider-Man his special powers. He is very strong, with a keen sense that warns of danger, and he can cling to almost any surface. Web shooters on his wrists spray out sticky webs, which harden in the air. Spider-Man uses his unique powers to catch criminals.

◀ THE NET-CASTING SPIDER

At night, the stick-like net-casting spider (*Dinopis*) hangs from a twig holding a very stretchy, sticky silk net. As insects crawl or fly past the tiny net is stretched wide to trap them. The spider has huge eyes to help it to see at night, hence the name ogre-faced spider. It makes a new net each evening, eating the old one even if it is unused.

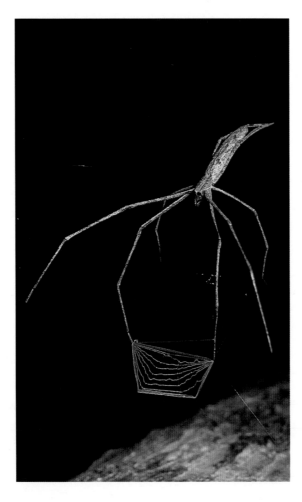

The net-casting spider hangs upside down, holding its elastic net in its front four legs. The legs are kept drawn in close to the body while the spider waits.

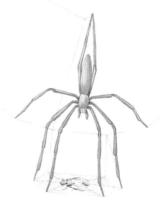

When an insect, such as an ant, scurries past, the spider opens the net and quickly drops down. It scoops up its meal then springs back up.

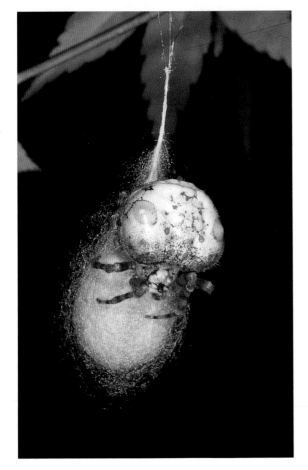

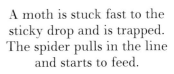

As a moth approaches, the bolas spider whirls the sticky droplet on the end of its fishing line.

A moth is stuck fast to the sticky drop and is trapped. The spider pulls in the line and starts to feed.

◄ FISHING FOR FOOD

This female bolas spider (*Mastophora*) is making a large egg case. Bolas spiders catch moths by using sticky balls on the end of a silk line. The spiders are named after the bolas (a strong cord connecting three balls) used by South American cowboys to trip up cattle. The spider produces a scent just like that made by female moths to draw male moths to its fishing line.

SPITTING SPIDER ►

This female spitting spider (*Scytodes*) is carrying a ball of eggs in her jaws. Spitting spiders produce glue as well as poison inside the poison glands in the front half of the body. When the spider is very close to its prey, it squirts out two lines of gummy poison from its fangs to pin down the victim. It then gives its prey a poisonous bite before tearing it free of the glue and eating its meal.

The spitting spider's fangs move from side to side as it squirts out its sticky poison. This imprisons the victim under two zigzag strands of quick-setting glue.

◄ SIMPLE NETS

The daddy-longlegs spider (*Pholcus*) spins a flimsy scaffold web that is almost invisible. When an insect, or another spider, gets tangled up in its web, the daddy-longlegs throws strands of fresh silk over its prey. It can do this from a distance because of its long legs. Once the victim is helpless, the spider moves in for the feast.

Catching Food

Only about half of all spiders spin webs to catch prey. Of the other half, some hide and surprise their victims with a sneak attack — crab spiders do this very well. Others, such as trapdoor spiders, set traps as well as ambushing prey. Many spiders, such as jumping spiders, are agile, fast-moving hunters that stalk their prey. Spiders are not usually very fussy about what they eat. Insects, such as grasshoppers, beetles, ants and bees are their main food, but some eat fish, while bigger spiders may catch mice and birds. Many spiders eat other spiders.

▲ SILK TRAPS

Orb webs are designed to catch insects up to about the size of the spiders that made them. This orb-web spider is eating a crane-fly. The prey has been bitten and wrapped in silk, then cut free from the web and carried away to be eaten. Some insects, such as moths, manage to escape from webs. Smaller spiders tend to free large insects from their webs before they do too much damage.

The empty shell of a partly eaten fly.

Dead flies wrapped in silk are left hanging for eating later.

◄ DAISY WEB

In the centre of this ox-eye daisy sits a green orb-web spider (*Araniella cucurbitina*). It has built its web over the middle of the daisy. Small flies, attracted to the innocent-looking flower, are trapped in the web. They end up as food for the spider who kills them, then crushes them to a pulp before sucking up a meal.

WATER HUNTER ▶

This fishing spider (*Dolomedes*) has caught a blue damselfly. It lives in swamps and pools where it sits on the leaves of water plants. It spreads its legs on the water's surface to detect ripples from insects that fall into the water, then rushes out to grab them. Fish swimming in the water below are also caught by this hunting spider. The spider may even dabble its legs in the water to attract small fish towards its waiting fangs.

◀ HAIRY HUNTER

Tarantulas are also called bird-eating spiders and they really do eat birds, although this one has caught a mouse. They also eat lizards, frogs and even small poisonous snakes. But most of the time, tarantulas feed on insects. They hunt at night, finding their prey by scent or by picking up vibrations with their sensitive hairs. After a quick sprint and a bite from powerful jaws, the spider can tuck into its meal. It may take as long as a day to suck the body of a snake dry.

ATHLETIC HUNTER ▶

Lynx spiders hunt their prey on plants. They sometimes jump from leaf to leaf after their prey, but at other times they sit and wait. The green lynx spider (*Peucetia*) is an athletic hunter with long spiny legs that enable it to leap easily from stem to stem. It often eats other spiders and is even a cannibal, eating members of its own species. This one has caught a termite.

Focus on Hunting

With bright, shiny colours like a peacock, large curious eyes like a cat and the agility to jump like a monkey, little jumping spiders are one of the most extraordinary spider families. Belonging to the family Salticidae, there are about 4,000 different kinds, many of which live in warmer parts of the world. Most jumping spiders are always on the prowl, darting jerkily along, peering all around for a possible meal. They can see in colour and form clear images of their prey. They stalk their prey rather like a cat stalks a mouse, crouching before the final pounce. Jumping spiders will turn their tiny heads to peer closely at a human face looking at them.

SIGN LANGUAGE
A male jumping spider's front legs are longer and thicker than a female's. He uses them in courtship dances, waving them about like sign language.

PREPARING TO LEAP
Before it jumps, the spider fixes itself firmly to a surface with a silk safety line. Then it leaps on to its target, pushing off with the four back legs. The Australian flying spider (*Satis volans*) also has wing-like flaps so it can glide during leaps.

STURDY LEGS
This female heavy jumper (*Hyllus giganteus*) is feeding on a leaf-hopper. A jumping spider's legs do not seem to be specially adapted for jumping. Their small size (less than 15mm long) and light weight probably help them to make amazing leaps.

Jumping Spiders

THE BIG LEAP

A jumping spider's strong front legs are often raised before a jump, stretched forwards in the air, and used to hold the prey when the spider lands. Scopulae (hairy tufts) on the feet help jumping spiders grip smooth and vertical surfaces. They can even leap away from a vertical surface to seize a flying insect.

JUMPING CANNIBALS

Jumping spiders will feed on their own relatives. This female two-striped jumping spider (*Telamonia dimidiata*) is feeding on another species of jumping spider. Some unusual *Portia* jumping spiders vibrate the webs of orb-weaving spiders, like an insect struggling to escape. When the orb-weaver comes out to investigate, the *Portia* spider pounces.

Hidden Traps

Some spiders do not go hunting for food. They prefer to lurk inside underground burrows or tubes of silk and wait for a meal to come by. Silk threads around the entrance to the burrow trip up passing insects and other small creatures. Inside the burrow, the spider feels the tug on its trip lines, giving it time to rush out and pounce on the prey before it can escape. Patient, lie-in-wait spiders include trapdoor spiders, which have special spines on their fangs to rake away the soil as they dig. The burrows also shelter spiders from the weather and help them to avoid enemies.

▲ SILK DOORS

The lid of a trapdoor spider's burrow is made of silk and soil with a silk hinge along one side. The door usually fits tightly into the burrow opening and may be camouflaged with sticks, leaves and moss. Where flooding occurs, walls or turrets are built around the entrance to keep out the water.

The spider waits for an insect to land on its tube-like web.

The spider spears the insect with its sharp jaws.

▲ A SILKEN TUBE

This purse-web spider (*Atypus affinis*) is shown outside its burrow. It usually lives inside a tubular purse of densely woven silk. The tube is about 45cm long and about the thickness of a finger. Part of it sticks up above the ground or from a tree trunk, and is well camouflaged with debris.

▲ INSIDE A PURSE-WEB

Inside its silken purse the spider waits for any insect to walk over the tube. It spears the insect through the tube with its sharp jaws and drags the prey inside.

▲ FUNNEL-WEB SPIDERS

The Sydney funnel-web (*Atrax robustus*) is one of the deadliest spiders in the world. It lives in an underground burrow lined with silk. From the mouth of the burrow is a funnel that can be up to 1m across. Trip wires leading from the funnel warn the spider that prey is coming. The spider can dig its own burrow with its fangs, but prefers to use existing holes and cracks. Funnel-web spiders eat mainly beetles, large insects, snails and small animals.

▲ TRIP WIRES

The giant trapdoor spider (*Liphistius*) may place silken trip lines around the entrance to its burrow to detect the movements of a passing meal. If it does not have trip lines, the spider relies on detecting the vibrations of prey through the ground. If it senses a meal is nearby, the spider rushes out of its burrow to grab the prey in its jaws.

Did you know? Trapdoor spiders may live for up to 20 years in their burrows.

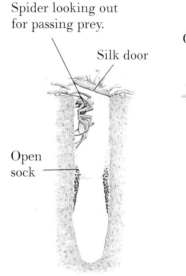

Spider looking out for passing prey.

Silk door

Centipede enters spider's burrow.

Open sock

False bottom of closed sock hides spider.

▲ ODD SPIDER OUT

Some unusual wolf spiders live in underground burrows. This tiger wolf spider (*Lycosa aspersa*) has dug out the soil with its fangs and lined the walls of its burrow with silk. To camouflage the entrance it has built a wall of twigs and litter.

▲ ALL KINDS OF TRAPS

Trapdoor spiders' burrows range from simple tubes to elaborate lairs with hidden doors and escape tunnels. The burrow of *Anidiops villosus* has a collapsible sock. The spider pulls it down to form a false bottom, hiding it from predators.

Spider Venom

Nearly all spiders use poison to kill or paralyse their prey and for defence. (Only spiders in the family Uloboridae have no poison glands.) Spider poison is called venom. It is injected into prey through fangs. There are two main kinds of venom that can have serious effects. Most dangerous spiders, such as widow spiders (*Lactrodectus*), produce nerve poison to paralyse victims quickly. The other kind of venom works more slowly, destroying tissues and causing ulcers and gangrene. It is made by the recluse spiders (*Loxosceles*). Spider venom is intended to kill insects and small prey – only about 30 spider species are dangerous to people.

▲ **VIOLIN SPIDER**
This small brown spider is one of the recluse spiders (*Loxosceles*). It lives in people's homes and may crawl into clothes and bedding. Bites from recluse spiders in America have caused ulcers, especially near the wound, and even death in humans.

▲ **WANDERING SPIDER**
The Brazilian wandering spider (*Phoneutria fera*) is a large hunting spider that produces one of the most toxic of all spider venoms. If disturbed it raises its front legs to expose its threatening jaws. It has the largest venom glands of any spider (up to 10mm long), which hold enough venom to kill 225 mice. Several people have died from this spider's bite.

The Spider Dance
In the Middle Ages people from Taranto in southern Italy called the large wolf spider Lycosa narbonensis *the tarantula. They believed the venom of this spider's bite could only be flushed from the body by doing the tarantella, a lively dance. However, Lycosa's bite is not serious. An epidemic of spider bites at the time was probably caused by the malmignatte spider* (Latrodectus tredecimguttatus).

▲ THE QUICK KILL

Crab spiders do not spin webs so they need to kill their prey quickly. They usually inject their venom into the main nerve cords in the neck where the poison will get to work most rapidly. They are able to kill insects much larger than themselves, such as bees.

◄ WIDOW SPIDER

The Australian red-back spider (*Latrodectus hasselti*) is one of the most deadly widow spiders. Widow spiders are named after the female's habit of eating the male after mating. Only female widow spiders are dangerous to people – the much smaller male's fangs are too tiny to penetrate human skin.

Did you know? A black widow's venom is 15 times more poisonous than a rattlesnake's.

▲ GENTLE GIANT

Tarantulas look very dangerous and have huge fangs, but at worst their bite is no more painful than a wasp sting. They have small venom glands and are unlikely to bite unless handled roughly. They use venom to digest their prey.

▲ BLACK WIDOW

The American black widow (*Latrodectus mactans*) is another spider with venom powerful enough to kill a person (although medicines can now prevent this happening). These shy spiders hide away if disturbed, but like to live near people. Of the main ingredients in their venom, one knocks out insects and another paralyses mammals and birds by destroying their nervous systems.

Fangs and Feeding

A spider's sharp, pointed fangs are part of its jaws. Each fang is like a curved, hollow needle. It is joined to a basal segment, which joins on to the spider's body just in front of the mouth. The fangs may be used for digging burrows and carrying eggs, but are mainly used for injecting venom and for defence. Venom passes through a tiny hole near the end of each fang. Although the fangs are not very long, the venom they deliver makes them into powerful weapons. Once prey is caught, a spider uses its jaws, palps and digestive juices to mash up its prey into a soggy, soupy lump. This is because a spider's mouth is too small for solid food. Then the spider sucks up the liquid food into its stomach. Its abdomen swells as the food is swallowed, so a spider looks fatter after a meal.

▲ **A SOGGY MEAL**

This garden spider (*Araneus diadematus*) has turned her prey into a soupy meal. The basal segments of the jaws often have jagged edges to help the spider tear and mash up its prey. Smaller jaws, called maxillae, on either side of the mouth are also used to turn prey into a liquid pulp.

FROG SOUP ▶

Spiders sometimes have to turn quite large items of food into pulp before they can suck up a meal. This rusty wandering spider (*Cupiennius getazi*) is turning a tree frog over and over to mash it up in its jaws. It finds the frogs by using the slit organs on its feet to detect the mating calls they make.

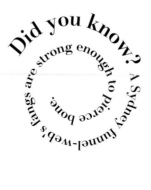

Did you know?
A Sydney funnel-web's fangs are strong enough to pierce bone.

40

DAGGER FANGS ▷

This tarantula's dagger-like fangs have pierced through the skin of a baby field mouse to inject venom into its body. The venom glands of tarantulas and trapdoor spiders are all inside the basal segments of the jaws. They do not extend into the head as in most other spiders. Tarantula venom can kill a small animal and causes burning and swelling in a person.

HOW FANGS WORK ▷

In most spiders, the fangs face each other and close together like pincers or pliers. In mygalomorph spiders (tarantulas and trapdoor spiders), however, the fangs stab downwards like two daggers. The spider has to raise its front end to strike forwards and down on to its prey. Prey needs to be on a firm surface such as the ground for these jaws to work.

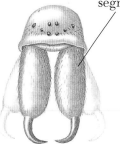

Basal segment

Fang

Pincer fangs swing together. They work well on webs and leaves.

Dagger fangs impale prey on the ground with a downwards action.

▲ FANGS FOR DEFENCE

An Australian trapdoor spider (*Aname*) tries to make itself look as frightening as possible if it is threatened. It tilts back its body and raises its front legs so that its long poisonous fangs are easy to see. It adopts this aggressive pose to warn an enemy to leave it alone.

▲ PINCER FANGS

The lobed argiope spider (*Argiope lobata*) has fangs that work like pincers. It catches large insects in its orb web and wraps them in silk before biting them. As in most spiders, the venom glands go well back inside the head.

Defence

Spiders are small, with soft bodies that make a tasty meal for many predators. To avoid their enemies, such as other spiders, hunting wasps, lizards and frogs, many spiders hide away. Trapdoor spiders hide in well-concealed burrows. Other spiders hide themselves by being beautifully camouflaged to blend in with their surroundings. In complete contrast, some spiders copy the bright colours of dangerous insects, such as wasps. This tricks enemies into leaving the spider alone. Spiders will even pretend to be dead, since predators prefer to eat live prey.

The spider raises its legs high up and waves them about to look more aggressive.

▼ THREATENING DISPLAY

The golden wheel spider (*Carparachne aureoflava*) lives on the sand dunes of the Namib Desert, southern Africa. Its gold colour blends in well with its surroundings. If caught out in the open, however, the spider rears up to make itself look large and more frightening to enemies.

By raising its abdomen high into the air, the spider makes itself appear larger.

Standing on tiptoe also helps to make it look larger.

ESCAPE WHEEL ▶

If the golden wheel spider's threatening display does not deter an enemy, it has another, remarkable way of escaping. The spider throws itself sideways, pulls in its legs and rolls itself into a ball. It then cartwheels rapidly away down the dunes.

HUNTING WASP ▷

This hunting wasp has just paralysed a spider with its sting. Most wasps that hunt spiders are solitary pompilid wasps. A wasp will attack spiders as large or larger than itself. First it stings the spider to paralyse it. Then it drags the spider off to a burrow, lays an egg on its body and buries the spider alive. When the egg hatches out, the wasp grub feeds on the spider meat. The spider provides a living larder for the grub as it grows.

▲ SPIDER ENEMIES

A hungry lizard crunches up a tasty spider meal. Many animals eat spiders, including frogs, toads, mice, shrews, monkeys, bandicoots and possums. Birds are not usually a threat, because most spiders are active at night when few birds are about. The most common enemies of spiders, however, are probably the smaller animals without backbones. These include other spiders, hunting wasps, assassin bugs, scorpions and centipedes.

Did you know? Daddy-long-legs spiders jump up and down to scare away enemies.

FIGHTING ON YOUR BACK ▷

This venomous spider throws itself on its back to display its warning colours when it is attacked. Colours such as yellow, orange, red and black are warning signals, saying "I am poisonous, leave me alone". Other active defence tactics include showing off the fangs and squirting liquid or venom at an attacker.

Bold markings on the underside warn enemies to leave this spider alone.

Colour and Camouflage

Is it a leaf, a twig or a piece of bark? Is it a bird dropping? No, it is a spider! Many spiders have bodies that are coloured and shaped just like objects in their surroundings. They are so well camouflaged that they are very hard to see, especially when they keep still. This allows the spider to sit out in the open where it can more easily catch food, yet remain invisible to its enemies and prey. A few spiders, such as crab spiders and some jumping spiders, can even change colour to match different backgrounds. It takes some time for the spider to do this, however. Brightly coloured spiders often taste nasty. These eye-catching colours warn enemies to leave them alone.

▲ ANT OR SPIDER?
The spear-jawed jumping spider (*Myrmarachne plataleoides*) looks just like an insect called a weaver ant. You can tell it is a spider because it has eight legs not six. It even waves its front legs like antennae to make the disguise more realistic. Spiders mimic ants because predators avoid ants' nasty stings.

▲ SAND SPIDER
When spiders are the same colour or pattern as their background they can be hard to spot. The wolf spider *Arctosa perita* lives on sand or gravel. Its speckled colouring breaks up the outline of its body so it is hard to see. Until it moves, the spider is almost invisible.

▲ LOOKING LIKE A FLOWER
With their colours matching all or part of a flower, many crab spiders lurk on the surface of plants waiting to catch insects. This is the seven-spined crab spider (*Epicadus heterogaster*). The fleshy lobes on its abdomen imitate the host plant's white, orchid-like flowers.

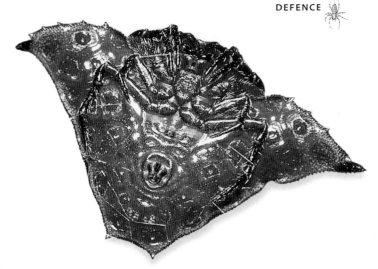

▲ LEAF LOOK-ALIKE

Spiders like this *Augusta glyphica* have lumpy or wrinkled abdomens. With their legs drawn up, they look just like a piece of dead leaf.

▲ BIRD DROPPING

Looking like a bird dropping is a very useful disguise for many spiders. Enemies are not likely to eat droppings and some insects are attracted to feed on the salts they contain. A few spiders even release a scent similar to bird droppings.

▲ TWIGGY DISGUISE

Spiders that look like twigs have to sit in a certain way to be well hidden. This *Poltys* spider sits with its front four legs held over its face and rear four pressed tightly against its abdomen. It looks like the jagged end of a broken twig when it keeps still.

Did you know? A South American wolf spider can change colour in 30 minutes.

LICHEN SPIDER ▶

The lichen huntsman (*Pandercetes gracilis*) from the rainforests of Australia and New Guinea spends all day pressed close to the bark of a tree. The spider's mottled colours match the colours of the lichens on the tree. Short hairs also give the colours a matt finish. All along its legs and the sides of its body, fringes of hair stop the spider casting a shadow.

Focus on

With broad, flat bodies and sideways scuttling movements like crabs, the members of the family Thomisidae are called crab spiders. There are about 3,000 species living all over the world. Crab spiders do not usually build webs. They often lie in wait for their prey on flowers, leaves, tree trunks or on the ground. Most are small (less than 20mm long) and rely on stealth and strong venom to catch prey. Males are often half the size of the females and their colours can be quite different.

BODY PARTS

Crab spiders are usually not very hairy and many, like this heather spider (*Thomisus onustus*), are brightly coloured. They often have wart-like lumps and bumps on their bodies, especially the females. The front pairs of legs are adapted for grasping prey.

COLOUR CHANGE

Female flower spiders (*Misumena vatia*) can change colour. A yellow pigment is moved from the intestines (gut) to the outer layer of the body to turn yellow and back again to turn white. It takes up to two days for the spider to complete the change.

BIG EATERS

Crab spiders can kill larger prey than themselves. This gold leaf crab spider (*Synema globosum*) has caught a honeybee. Its venom is powerful, quickly paralysing the bee. This avoids a long struggle, which might damage the spider and draw the attention of enemies.

Crab Spiders

SIX-SPOT CRAB SPIDER
The unusual six-spot crab spider (*Platythomisus sexmaculatus*) has very striking markings. These might be warning colours, but very little is known about this spider. No one has ever seen a male six-spot crab spider. The female, shown here, is about 15mm long in real life.

Eight small eyes give quite good vision.

A crab spider's front two pairs of legs are longer and sturdier than the rest.

THE AMBUSH
This flower spider (*Misumena vatia*) has sat on a daisy for several days. It hardly moved as it waited to ambush an insect, such as a bee. The two rear pairs of legs anchored the spider firmly on to the flower. The two front pairs of legs, armed with bristles, grabbed the bee like pincers.

FEEDING TIME
This common crab spider (*Xysticus cristatus*) is eating a dance fly. Crab spiders do not store prey like many other spiders. They can only deal with one meal at a time. Insects can pass close by a feeding crab spider unnoticed. A crab spider's jaws have no teeth and cannot mash up its prey. Instead, fangs inject digestive juices that break down the prey's insides. The spider sucks up its liquid meal, leaving a dry, empty husk behind.

Males and Females

Most spiders spend much of their life alone, only coming together to mate. Females often look different from males. The female is usually larger because she needs to carry a lot of eggs inside her body. She also has extra glands to make a silk covering for her eggs. The female may even guard the eggs and young spiderlings after they hatch. She is also usually a drab colour to help hide her and her young from enemies. The male, on the other hand, takes no part in looking after his family after mating. He is usually smaller and sometimes more colourful. Males often have longer legs to help search for a mate.

▲ **SPERM WEB**
This male garden spider (*Araneus diadematus*) is filling his palps with sperm before searching for a mate. He has made a small web and squirted some sperm on to it. He sucks up the sperm into the swollen tip of each palp.

▲ **MALE MEALS?**
The much larger female black widow spider (*Latrodectus mactans*) sometimes eats the smaller, brown male after mating. Other female spiders occasionally do this, too. The most dangerous time for many males, however, is before mating. If the female is not ready to mate or does not recognize the male's signals, she may eat the male before he has a chance to mate.

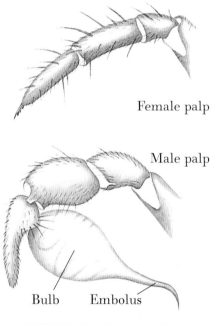

Female palp

Male palp

Bulb   Embolus

▲ **DIFFERENT PALPS**
Males have larger palps than females. The embolus on the tip of a male's palp is used to suck up sperm into the bulb. It pumps sperm out into the female's body during mating.

◄ EGG CARRIER

This female *Sosippus mimus* is spinning a silk cocoon to protect her eggs. The number of eggs laid by a female spider usually depends on her size. Some tiny spiders, such as *Atrophonysia intertidalis*, lay only one egg, while large *Nephila* spiders lay 1,000 or more. A spider's abdomen has a fairly thin covering, so it can stretch a great deal when a female has many eggs developing inside.

SPOT THE DIFFERENCE ►

This male and female ladybird spider (*Eresus niger*) show very clearly the differences between some male and female spiders. Their difference in size varies a great deal, but adult females can be over three times the size of males. The female is well camouflaged in a velvety blue-black skin, while the male looks like a brightly-coloured ladybird. He will run across open ground in search of a mate in spring. She usually hides away under stones.

Female ladybird spider (maximum body length up to 35mm)

Male ladybird spider (maximum body length up to 10mm)

Did you know? Female *Nephila* spiders can weigh 1,000 times more than the males.

LITTLE AND LARGE ►

A tiny male giant orb-weaver (*Nephila maculata*) mates with a huge female. They look so different it is hard to believe that they are the same species. The very small size of the male helps him to avoid being eaten by the female, since he is smaller than her usual prey. The female has two openings on her underside to receive sperm from the male's palps.

Focus on

Female spiders attract males by giving off a special scent called a pheromone. Each species has a different pheromone, to help the males find the right mate. Once he has found a female, the male has to give off the right signals so that the female realizes he is not a meal. Courtship signals include special dances, drumming, buzzing, or plucking the female's web in a particular way. Some males distract the females with a gift of food while others tie up the females with strands of silk before mating.

NOISY COURTSHIP

The male buzzing spider (*Anyphaena accentuata*) beats his abdomen against a leaf to attract a mate. The sound is loud enough for people to hear. He often buzzes on the roof of the female's oak-leaf nest. Other male hunting spiders make courtship sounds by rubbing one part of their bodies against another.

The male presents a gift to the female.

MATING SUCCESS

The male grass funnel-weaver (*Agelena labyrinthica*) is almost as large as the female and can be quite aggressive. He taps his palps on her funnel web to announce his arrival. If the female is ready to mate, she draws in her legs and collapses as if she is paralysed.

BEARING GIFTS

A male nursery-web spider (*Pisaura mirabilis*) presents an insect gift to the female. He has neatly gift-wrapped his present in a dense covering of very shiny white silk. Once the female has accepted his gift and is feeding, the male can mate with her in safety.

Courtship

COURTSHIP DANCES

Spiders that can see well at a distance often dance together before mating. This wolf spider (*Lycosa*) waves his palps like semaphore flags to a female in the distance. Male spiders also strike special poses and use their long, stout front legs to make signalling more effective.

A RISKY BUSINESS

Male garden spiders (*Araneus*) often have great difficulty courting a female. They are usually much smaller and lighter than the female and have to persuade her to move on to a special mating thread. The male joins the mating thread to the edge of the female's web. He tweaks the silk strands of her web to lure the female towards him.

COURTSHIP PROBLEMS

This male green orb-weaver (*Araniella cucurbitina*) has lost four legs in the courtship process. When the female attacked him, he swung down a silken dragline. He will climb back up again when it is safe.

JUMPING SPIDERS

This pair of jumping spiders (*Salticus*) are ready to mate. Male jumping spiders impress females by twirling and waltzing, waving their legs, palps and abdomens. Females often attract more than one male and they have to compete to mate with her. The female reaches out and touches the male when she is ready to mate.

Spider Eggs

Female spiders usually lay their eggs a week or two after mating, although some spiders wait several months. Not all the eggs are laid at once and many spiders lay several batches, usually at night when it is safer. The female may lay from one to over 1,000 eggs per batch. Most spiders lay their eggs on a circle of silk together with some of the male's stored sperm. It is not until now that the eggs are fertilized. The outer layer of the eggs gradually hardens and the female spins a cocoon around them for extra protection.

Ananse the Spider Man

A hero of many folk tales in West Africa and the Caribbean is Ananse. He is both a spider and a man. When things are going well he is a man, but in times of danger he becomes a

spider. Ananse likes to trick the other animals and get the better of those who are much bigger than himself. He may be greedy and selfish, but he is also funny. He is a hero because he brought the gift of telling stories to people.

◀ IN DISGUISE

To hide their eggs from hungry predators, spiders may camouflage the cocoons with plant material, insect bodies, mud or sand. This scorpion spider (*Arachnura*) hangs her brown egg cases from her web like a string of rubbish, then poses as a dead leaf beneath them. Other spiders hide egg cases under stones or bark, or fix leaves together like a purse.

▲ SPINNING THE COCOON

A *Nephila edulis* spins her egg cocoon. She uses special strong, loopy silk that traps a lot of air and helps to stop the eggs drying out. Her eggs are covered with a sticky coating to fix them to the silk. The final protective blanket of yellow silk will turn green, camouflaging the cocoon.

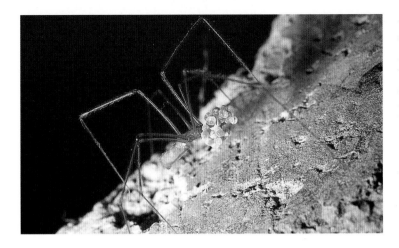

FLIMSY EGG CASE

The daddy-longlegs spider (*Pholcus*) uses hardly any silk for her egg case. Just a few strands hold the eggs loosely together. Producing a large egg case uses up a lot of energy and females with large egg cases often have shrunken bodies. The daddy-longlegs carries the eggs around in her jaws. She is unable to feed until the eggs hatch.

SILK NEST

The woodlouse spider (*Dysdera crocota*) lays her eggs in a silken cell under the ground. She also lives in this shelter, where she is safer from enemies. At night, the woodlouse spider emerges from its silken house to look for woodlice, which it kills with its enormous fangs.

CAREFUL MOTHER

A green lynx spider (*Peucetia*) protects her egg case on a cactus. She fixes the case with silk lines, like a tent's guy ropes, and drives off any enemies. If necessary, she cuts the silk lines and lets the egg case swing in mid-air, balancing on top like a trapeze artist. If she has to move her eggs to a safer place, she drags the case behind her with silk threads.

GUARD DUTY

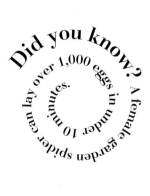

Did you know? A female garden spider can lay over 1,000 eggs in under 10 minutes.

Many female spiders carry their eggs around with them. This rusty wandering spider (*Cupiennius getazi*) carries her egg sac attached to her spinnerets. Spiders that do this often moisten the eggs in water and sunbathe to warm them and so speed up their development.

Spiderlings

Most spider eggs hatch within a few days or weeks of being laid. The spiderlings (baby spiders) do not usually have any hairs, spines, claws or colour when they first hatch. They feed on the egg yolk stored in their bodies and grow fast. They cast off their first skin in a process called moulting. Spiderlings have to moult several times as they grow into adults. After the first moult, young spiders look like tiny versions of their parents. Most baby spiders look after themselves from the moment of hatching, but some mothers guard and feed their young until they leave the nest. Male spiders do not look after their young at all.

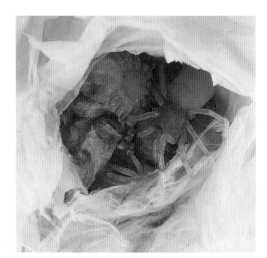

▲ **HATCHING OUT**

These spiderlings are emerging from their egg case. Spiderlings may stay inside the case for some time after hatching. Some spiders have an egg tooth to help break them out of the egg, but mother spiders may also help their young to hatch. Spiderlings from very different species look similar..

◀ **NURSERY WEB**

Female nursery-web spiders (*Pisaura mirabilis*) build a silk tent for their egg cases when they are ready to hatch. The mother sits on the tent and guards the eggs and hatchlings for a week or so. The baby spiders moult once and then gradually leave the nest to start life on their own.

Nursery-web spider guarding her nest

Nursery tent

Egg case

▲ **A SPIDER BALL**

Garden spiderlings (*Araneus*) stay together for several days after hatching. They form small gold and black balls that break apart if danger threatens, but re-form when danger has passed.

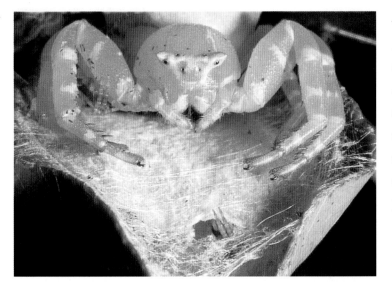

◀ BABY BODIES

A female crab spider watches over her young as they hatch out. Spider eggs contain a lot of yolk, which provides a good supply of energy for the baby spiders. They are well developed when they hatch out, with the same body shape and number of legs as adults. Baby spiders, however, cannot produce silk or venom until their first moult.

BABY CARRIER ▶

Pardosa wolf spiders carry their egg cases joined to their spinnerets. When the eggs are ready to hatch, the mother tears open the case and the babies climb on to her back. If the spiderlings fall off, they can find their way back by following silk lines the mother trails behind her.

Spiderlings cling to special hairs on their mother's back for about a week.

Spotted wolf spider
(*Pardosa amentata*)

Silk threads are called gossamer.

Did you know? Many young spiders often feed on their own mother's body.

▲ FOOD FROM MUM

The mothercare spider (*Theridion sisyphium*) feeds her young on food brought up from her stomach. The rich soup is made of digested insects and cells lining her gut. The babies shake her legs to beg for food. They grow faster than babies that feed themselves.

▲ BALLOON FLIGHT

Many spiderlings take to the air to find new places to live or to avoid being eaten by their brothers and sisters. On a warm day with light winds, they float through the air on strands of silk drawn out from their spinnerets. This is called ballooning.

Moulting

Spiders do not grow gradually, like we do. Instead they grow in a series of steps. At each step, the spider grows a new outer skin, or exoskeleton, under the old one and moults (sheds) the old one. Lost or damaged legs and other body parts can be replaced during a moult. Small spiders moult in a few hours, but larger spiders may need several days. A young spider moults about five to ten times as it grows into an adult. A few spiders continue to moult throughout their adult lives.

▲ **COLOUR CHANGE**
Adult spiders that have just moulted are quite pale for a while and do not show their true colours for a day or so. The fangs of this newly moulted tarantula have no colour as yet.

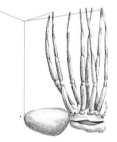

1 The first split forms along the carapace.

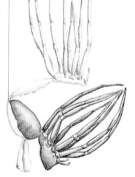

2 The split moves back along the abdomen.

3 Carefully the spider heaves its body out of the old skin.

4 The spider expands its body to stretch the new skeleton.

▲ **STAGES IN MOULTING**
The main stages in the moulting process of a spider are shown above. It is a dangerous process. Legs can get broken and spiders are vulnerable to enemies as they moult since they cannot defend themselves or run away.

▲ **THE OLD SKIN**
This is the old exoskeleton of a fishing spider (*Dolomedes*). The piece at the top is the lid of the carapace. The holes are where the legs fitted inside the skin.

HOW MANY MOULTS? ▶

This young red and white spider (*Enoplognatha ovata*) is in the middle of moulting. It is hiding under a leaf out of sight of enemies. A larger adult spider seems to have come to investigate. It is not until the final moult that a spider takes on its adult colours. Most spiders stop moulting when they become adults. Smaller species need fewer moults to reach adult size. Males also go through fewer moults than females because they are smaller when fully grown.

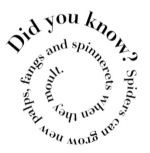

◀ MOULTING PROCESS

A tarantula pulls itself free of its old skin. Before a spider moults, it stops feeding and rests for a while. During this time, a new wrinkled exoskeleton forms underneath the old one and part of the old skin is absorbed back into the body to be recycled. The spider then pumps blood into the front of its body, making it swell and split the old skin, which is now very thin.

Did you know? Spiders can grow new palps, fangs and spinnerets when they moult.

A NEW SKIN ▶

This Chilean rose tarantula (*Grammostola cala*) moulted recently. Its new skin is bright and colourful. It looks very hairy because new hairs have replaced those that have been lost or damaged. When a spider first escapes from its old skin, it flexes its legs to make sure the joints stay supple. As the new skeleton dries out, it hardens. The skin on the abdomen stays fairly stretchy, so it can expand as the spider eats, or fill with eggs in females.

57

Spiders Everywhere

From mountain tops, caves and deserts to forests, marshes and grasslands, there are few places on Earth without spiders. Even remote islands are inhabited by spiders, perhaps blown there on the wind or carried on floating logs. Many spiders are quite at home in our houses and some travel the world on cargo ships. Many spiders live on sewage works, where there are plenty of flies for them to feed on. Spiders are not very common in watery places, however, since they cannot breathe underwater. There are also no spiders in Antarctica, although they do manage to live on the edge of the Arctic. To survive the winter in cool places, spiders may stay as eggs, hide away under grass, rocks or bark or make nests together. Some even have a type of antifreeze to stop their bodies freezing up.

▲ **HEDGEROW WEBS**
One of the most common spiders on bushes and hedges in Europe and Asia is the hammock web (*Linyphia triangularis*). One hedge may contain thousands of webs with their haphazard threads.

Did you know? Some spiders live in the web of another species and steal its food.

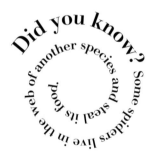

◄ **SPIDER IN THE SINK**
The spiders that people sometimes find in the sink or the bath are usually male house spiders (*Tegenaria*) that have fallen in while searching for a mate. They cannot climb back up the smooth sides because they do not have gripping tufts of hair on their feet like hunting spiders.

▲ CAVE SPIDER

The cave orb-weaver (*Meta menardi*) almost always builds its web in very dark places, often suspended from the roof. It is found in caves, mines, hollow trees, railway tunnels, drains, wells and the corners of outbuildings in Europe, Asia and North America.

▲ DESERT SPIDER

The main problem for desert spiders such as this white lady (*Leucorhestris arenicola*) is the lack of water. It hides away from the intense heat in a burrow beneath the sand and, in times of drought, may go into suspended animation. Desert spiders live in different places to avoid competition for food.

◄ SEASHORE SPIDER

This beach wolf spider (*Arctosa littoralis*) is well camouflaged on the sand. It lives in a very hostile place. Waves pound on the beach and shift the sand, there is little fresh water and the sun quickly dries everything out. There is little food, although insects gather on seaweed, rocks and plants growing along the edge of the shore.

RAINFOREST SPIDER ►

The greatest variety of spiders is to be found in the rainforests of the tropics. Here the climate is warm all year round and plenty of food is always available. This forest huntsman (*Pandercetes plumipes*) is well camouflaged against a tree trunk covered in lichen. To hide, it presses its body close against the tree. It lives in Malaysia where it is found in gardens as well as the rainforest.

59

Focus on

No spiders live in the open sea, but several hunt in and around fresh water. If they sense danger, they dive down underwater by holding on to plants. Only one spider, the water spider (*Argyroneta aquatica*), spends its whole life underwater. It lives in ponds, lakes and slow-moving streams in Europe and Asia. It still needs to breathe oxygen from the air, so it lives in a bubble of air called a diving bell. It does not need a regular supply of food because its body works very slowly. It catches prey by sticking its legs out of the diving bell to pick up vibrations in the water.

FOOD FROM THE WATER

This fishing spider (*Dolomedes fimbriatus*) has caught a colourful reed-frog. Fishing spiders also eat tadpoles, small fish and insects that have fallen into the water. Their venom paralyses their prey very quickly, so it has little chance of escape.

FISHING FOR FOOD

Fishing spiders sit on floating leaves or twigs with their front legs resting on the surface of the water. Hairs on their legs detect ripples. The spider can work out the position of prey from the direction and distance between the ripples. Ripples from twigs or leaves falling into the water often confuse the spider.

Water Spiders

DINING TABLE

Neither water spiders nor fishing spiders can eat in the water, because it would dilute their digestive chemicals. Water spiders feed inside their diving bells, while fishing spiders have their meals on the bank or an object floating in the water. This fishing spider is eating a stickleback on a mossy bank. The tail of the fish is caught in the sticky tentacles of a sundew plant.

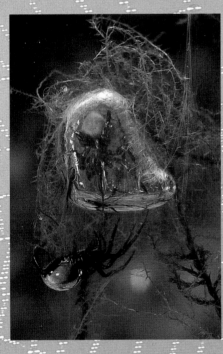

1 To make a diving bell, the water spider spins a web fixed to an underwater plant. Then it swims to the surface to trap a bubble of air, which it carries down to the web.

2 The spider releases the bubble, which floats up to be trapped inside the roof of the web. To fill the diving bell with air takes up to six trips to and from the surface.

3 Once the bell is finished, the spider eats, mates and lays its eggs inside. This male spider is visiting a female. She will only leave her bell to collect more air or catch food.

Spider Families

To help them study spiders, scientists divide the 35,000 known species into three groups, known as suborders. The three groups are: araneomorphs (true spiders), mygalomorphs (tarantulas, purse-web spiders and trapdoor spiders) and the rare liphistiomorphs (giant trapdoor spiders). Most spiders are araneomorphs with jaws that close together sideways. These groups are further divided into 105 families. Spiders are put in families according to such things as the arrangement of their eyes, their silk-making glands or the number of claws on their feet. Some of the larger families, as well as the rarest, are shown here.

Giant trapdoor spider
(*Liphistius desultor*)

▲ **GIANT TRAPDOOR SPIDERS**
The Liphistiomorphs are rare spiders that live in Southeast Asia and Japan. There are about 20 different species. They live in burrows with trapdoor entrances. These very primitive spiders have bands across their abdomens and may look more like spiders that lived millions of years ago.

Money spider
(*Linyphia montana*)

▲ **MONEY SPIDERS**
The Linyphiidae is the second largest spider family with about 3,700 species. Linyphiids are usually very small and are commonly called money spiders. They are by far the commonest spiders in cooler, temperate parts of the world. They build hammock webs and hang upside-down beneath them.

▲ **ORB-WEB SPIDERS**
The main family of orb-weavers is the Araneidae with about 2,600 species. A typical member is this Jamaican orb-weaver (*Argiope*). It has a stout body with a rounded abdomen and sits in the centre of its circular web. Garden spiders belong to this family.

HUNTSMAN SPIDERS ▶

The Sparassidae (also called Heteropodidae) huntsman spiders are a family of about 1,000 species. Most live in tropical regions where they are sometimes called giant crab spiders. The Australian huntsman is one of the largest members with a body length of over 30mm. Some species of this family have been discovered in crates of bananas.

Australian Huntsman
(Isopeda)

Classification Chart

Kingdom	**Animalia**	(all animals)
Phylum	**Arthropoda**	(animals with exoskeletons and jointed legs)
Class	**Arachnida**	(arthropods with eight legs)
Order	**Araneae**	(spiders)
Suborder	**Araneomorphae**	(true spiders)
Family	**Theridiidae**	(comb-footed spiders)
Genus	*Latrodectus*	(widow spiders)
Species	*Mactaus*	(black widow spider)

◀ SPIDER NAMES

Scientists classify (group) every spider and give it a Latin name. This chart shows how the black widow spider is classified. Few spiders have common names and these vary from country to country. Their Latin name, however, stays the same all over the world.

Did you know? The first spiders lived about 400 million years ago on Earth.

Black spotted jumper
(Acragus)

◀ JUMPING SPIDERS

The world's largest spider family is the Salticidae containing over 4,000 species of jumping spiders. These small, active daylight hunters have large front eyes and an amazing ability to stalk and jump on prey. They mostly live in tropical areas and many are brightly coloured.

▲ CRAB SPIDERS

Another very large family is the Thomisidae with about 3,000 species of crab spiders. Crab spiders are found all over the world. They do not usually build webs and many sit waiting on flowers or leaves to ambush prey. They often rely on good camouflage to blend in with their surroundings and avoid predators.

Spider Relatives

Spiders belong to a large group of animals called arthropods (the word means jointed foot). Other arthropods include crabs, prawns, woodlice, centipedes and insects. Spiders are also members of a smaller group of animals with eight legs called arachnids. Other arachnids include scorpions, mites, ticks and harvestmen. Spiders are different from other arachnids because they have silk glands in the abdomen. Mites produce silk from the mouth and pseudoscorpions from the jaws. Spiders are also the only arachnids to inject venom with fangs. Scorpions have a stinging tail and pseudoscorpions have venom in their palps.

▲ **CAMEL SPIDER**

This scorpion is fighting a camel spider. People once thought camel spiders could kill camels, but they are not even poisonous. They have big, powerful jaws and are fast runners. They usually live in dry places feeding on insects. Camel spiders are also called solifugids, wind scorpions and sun spiders.

Scorpions use their large pincers to grab, crush and tear prey, which is then passed to the jaws.

The sting is used to subdue prey and in self-defence.

The exoskeleton is like tough leathery armour.

Fine bristles on the legs are sensitive to vibrations.

◄ **SCORPION**

Scorpions are much larger than most spiders. They have two large pincer-like palps at the front and a narrow tail with a poisonous sting at the rear. Some scorpions can kill people, though they sting mainly in self-defence. Young scorpions are born alive and are carried on their mother's back for two to four weeks.

▲ WHIP SPIDER

The closest relatives of spiders may be the whip spiders, such as this *Damon variegatus*. The first pair of legs are very long, like whips. They are used for sensing prey at a distance, not for walking. Unlike spiders, whip spiders have an abdomen divided into segments and palps like pincers for grabbing their prey. They hunt at night, but are not poisonous.

▲ VELVET MITE

These tiny spider relatives do not have bodies divided into two parts, like spiders. Many feed on plants and are serious pests. Other mites are parasites, feeding off much larger animals.

Did you know? Some scorpions have special light-sensitive cells in their tails.

▲ SEA SPIDER

In spite of their name, sea spiders are not spiders at all. They used to be grouped with the arachnids, but are now put in a separate class of their own and are probably not closely related. Sea spiders have a tiny body with four, five or six pairs of long, spindly legs. Some live in the freezing waters off the coast of Antarctica. This one is from Tasmania.

HARVESTMAN ▲

Often called harvest spiders, these long-legged arachnids are common around harvest time. They use their long legs to detect and trap insects, since they have no poison or silk glands.

The body of a harvestman is in one piece and it has only two eyes on a turret near the middle of the body. To protect itself from predators, a harvestman gives off a nasty smell.

Spiders and People

Most people are scared of spiders. With their long legs, hairy bodies and a habit of lurking in dark corners, spiders have not made themselves popular. Yet they are truly fascinating animals. Only a handful are dangerous to people and medicines, called antivenins, can now help people recover quickly from a deadly spider's bite. Many spiders are useful in helping to control insect pests not only on crops and in gardens, but also in our homes. In most countries it is bad luck to kill a spider, but people are their greatest threat. We destroy their habitats and reduce their numbers in the wild by collecting spiders to be sold as pets.

▲ **FEAR OF SPIDERS**
This man is obviously unafraid of spiders. He is quite happy to have a tarantula walk over his face. Some experts think that we are born with a fear of spiders. This may be because a few spiders were dangerous to our ancestors in the distant past when we lived closer to nature.

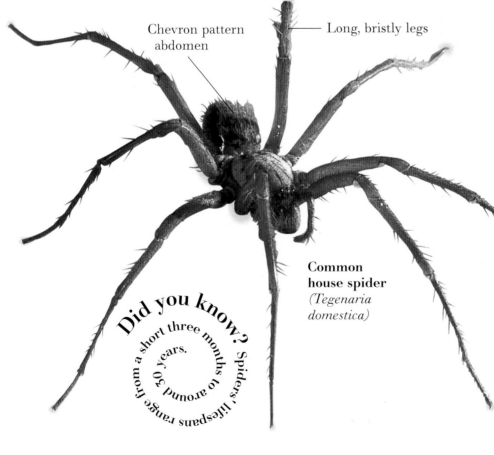

Chevron pattern abdomen

Long, bristly legs

Common house spider
(Tegenaria domestica)

Did you know? Spiders' lifespans range from a short three months to around 30 years.

◀ **HOUSE SPIDERS**
In cooler, temperate countries, house spiders *(Tegenaria)* are some of the commonest spiders. The common house spider leaves unwelcome, dusty sheet webs, called cobwebs, in the corners of rooms and against windows. A maze of trip wires over the surface of the web traps earwigs, flies and other household pests. House spiders may live for several years in the shelter of our homes.

HABITATS IN DANGER

People destroy and pollute the places in which spider and many other animals live. Clearing tropical rainforests, such as this one in Paraguay, South America, is particularly destructive. A huge variety of species of spiders live in the rainforest, many of them not yet known to scientists.

Little Miss Muffett

Miss Muffett was the daughter of the Reverend Thomas Muffett, a spider expert. When she was ill, her father made her eat crushed spiders as a cure. This made her terrified of spiders. A fear of spiders is called arachnophobia.

SPIDERS IN MEDICINE

This Piaroa shaman (medicine man) from Venezuela, South America, uses a tarantula hunting mask as part of a ceremony. In Europe and America, spiders have been used in the past to treat malaria, plague, toothache and headache. Sometimes the spiders were hung in a bag around the neck or eaten.

Ladybird spider
(Eresus niger)

RARE SPIDERS

Fewer than 20 species of spiders around the world are listed as threatened with extinction. They include the ladybird spider shown here. There must be, however, hundreds or even thousands more spiders in danger that we do not know about yet. Spiders need our protection. For example, the Mexican red-knee tarantula (*Brachypelma smithi*) is now rare in the wild because of over-collection by the pet trade. Spiders that have been bred in captivity may help this species to survive.

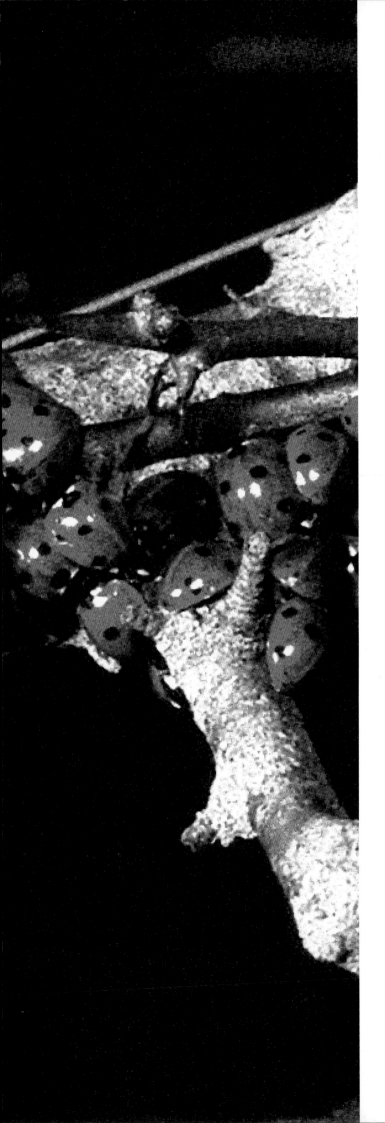

BEETLES AND BUGS

Some people call all insects 'bugs', but to a scientist, bugs are just one group of insects. Bugs have piercing and sucking mouthparts to suck plant sap or insect body juices. There are at least 55,000 different kinds of bugs, including blood-sucking assassin bugs and bedbugs, singing cicadas, lantern bugs and shield bugs. The biggest group of insects are beetles, which have biting jaws instead of sucking mouthparts. They include long-nosed weevils, spotted ladybirds, tiger beetles, diving beetles and fireflies. Other groups of insects covered in this section of the book are flies, dragonflies, fleas, grasshoppers, earwigs, cockroaches, stick insects, caddisflies and lice.

Nature's Success Story

If you were an alien visiting Earth, which creature would you consider the main life form? We humans like to think we dominate Earth, but insects are far more successful. There are over one million different species (kinds) of insects, compared to just one human species.

Scientists divide insects into groups called orders. The insects in each order share certain features. Beetles and bugs are two major insect orders. The main difference between them is that beetles have biting jaws and bugs have sucking mouthparts. Beetles are the largest order of all. So far, 350,000 different kinds of beetles and 55,000 different kinds of bugs have been found.

Long antennae give longhorn beetles their name.

Eyes on the front of the head give very accurate vision.

All beetles have biting jaws, located on the underside of the head.

Jointed legs.

Spotted longhorn beetle (*Strangalia maculata*)

Hard wing cases protect delicate rear wings.

▲ THE BEETLE ORDER

Beetles belong to the order Coleoptera, which means 'sheath wings'. Most beetles have two pairs of wings. The tough front wings fold over the delicate rear wings to form a hard, protective sheath, like body armour. Longhorn beetles owe their name to their long antennae (feelers), which look like long horns.

◄ LIVING IN WATER

Not all beetles and bugs live on land. Some, like this diving beetle (*Dytiscus marginalis*), live in fresh water. The diving beetle hunts underwater, diving down to look for food on the stream bed.

◄ FEEDING TOGETHER

A group of aphids feeds on a plant stem, sucking up liquid sap. Most beetles and bugs live alone, but a few species, such as aphids, gather together in large numbers. Although they do not form a community, as ants and bees do, living in a group does give some protection from predators.

What's in a Name?
This image comes from the animated feature film A Bug's Life. *The hero of the cartoon is not actually a bug at all, but an ant. True bugs are a particular group of insects with sucking mouthparts that can slurp up liquid food.*

Forest shield bug
(*Pentatoma rufipes*)

Six legs keep the bug stable as it scurries along the ground.

Antennae for touching and smelling.

Thin wing-tip.

Hard wing base.

◄ THE BUG ORDER

Bugs come in many shapes and sizes. All have long, jointed mouthparts that form a tube through which they suck up liquid food, like a syringe. Their order name is Hemiptera, which means 'half-wings'. The name refers to the front wings of many bugs, such as shield bugs, which are hard at the base and flimsy at the tip. With their wings closed, shield bugs are shaped like a warrior's shield.

Tube-like mouthparts under the insect's head.

Eyes on the front of the head.

THE YOUNG ONES ►

Young beetles, called grubs or larvae, look very different from adult beetles. A young cockchafer (*Melolontha melolontha*) feeds on plant roots in the soil. Almost all young beetles and bugs hatch from eggs. They pass through several stages in their life cycle.

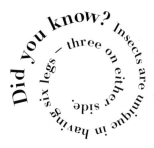

Did you know? Insects are unique in having six legs – three on either side.

All Kinds of Beetles

One in every five animals on Earth is a beetle. These insects owe much of their success to their natural body armour, which protects them against attack. Beetles are found all over the world, except in Antarctica and in the oceans. Long-nosed weevils, ground beetles, ladybirds, scarabs and glowing fireflies are all major beetle groups.

◄▲ LARGEST AND SMALLEST
Beetles come in various sizes. Goliath beetles from Africa (left) are the largest beetles, and one of the largest insects of all. They grow up to 15cm in length and weigh up to 100g. At the other end of the scale, feather-winged beetles are tiny – under 1mm long and smaller than a pinhead. Hairy-winged dwarf beetles are only 0.25mm long. The tiny beetles (above) are foraging in a flower.

Goliath beetle
(Goliathus goliatus)

Hercules beetle
(Dynastes hercules)

SCARY SIGHT ▶
Hercules beetles are named after the Classical Roman hero Hercules, who was famous for his strength. The tough, curved cuticle on the male's head forms huge horns, which he uses to fight and frighten away other males.

Desert scarab
(Scarabidae)

Weevil
(Curculionidae)

▲ LONG-NOSED WEEVILS

Weevils are the largest family of beetles. There are over 40,000 species. They are also called snout beetles, because of their long noses that scientists call rostrums. The beetle's jaws, and sometimes its eyes, are found at the tip of the long snout. The antennae are often positioned halfway down the beetle's rostrum.

▲ BRIGHT AND BEAUTIFUL

This beetle is a desert scarab from western USA. There are more than 20,000 species in the scarab family alone. Most are brown, black, green or red, but some are gold, blue, rainbow-coloured or plain white. Scarab beetles are an important part of the food chain because they eat dung, returning its nutrients to the soil.

Fiddle beetle
(*Mormolycei phyllodes*)

Trilobite beetle
(*Duliticola*)

◀ FLAT AS A PANCAKE

Beetles have evolved many differently shaped bodies to help them survive. The amazing fiddle beetle comes from Malaysia. As its name suggests, the beetle is shaped like a violin. Fiddle beetles are almost flat, which helps them slip between the flat bracket fungi on the trees in which they live.

▲ SPINY SHAPE

Trilobite beetles live in the rainforests of Borneo, in south-east Asia. With their flattened, scaly bodies, they resemble trilobites, a group of armoured sea-creatures that died out millions of years ago. Unlike most insects, trilobite beetles do not have wings and cannot fly away to escape their enemies. However, the sharp spines on their bodies keep most predators at bay.

Bugs of Every Kind

Like beetles, bugs live on every continent except Antarctica. They are found both on dry land and in fresh water. They are so small that they are rarely noticed by people and can survive on very little food. All bugs have piercing and sucking mouthparts, which are tucked beneath their heads when not in use. Many bugs suck juicy sap from plants. Some hunt other insects and suck their juices instead.

Bugs are made up of two large groups. True bugs form one group, whose scientific name is Heteroptera, meaning 'different wings'. Their front wings have hard bases and thin tips. True bugs include water stick insects, assassin bugs, shield bugs and bedbugs. Other bugs belong to the group Homoptera, which means 'same wings'. These bugs have one or two pairs of wings that are the same texture all over. They include leafhoppers, aphids, scale insects and cicadas.

Cicada
(Cicadidae family)

▲ BIGGEST AND SMALLEST
Cicadas are one of the largest bugs, growing up to 5cm long with a wingspan of up to 15cm. Giant water bugs, also called 'toe-biters', grow up to 12cm long. The whitefly is one of the smallest bugs – at only 1mm long, it is almost too tiny to be seen by the naked human eye.

Scale insects
(Coccoidae)

Shield bug
(*Palomena prasina*)

STRANGE INSECTS ▶
Like beetles, bugs vary a lot in shape. Scale insects owe their name to the hard scale that covers and protects the body of the females. Scale insects are unusual bugs. Most adult females have no legs, wings or antennae, and don't look like insects at all! The males have wings but no scale and look rather like tiny midges.

▲ CROSSED WINGS
Shield bugs have broad, flattened bodies. This species is dull in colour, but some are bright scarlet, blue or green. When resting, the shield bug crosses its front wings over its back so that its wing-tips overlap. From above, the wings form an X-shape by which you can identify true bugs – the Heteroptera group.

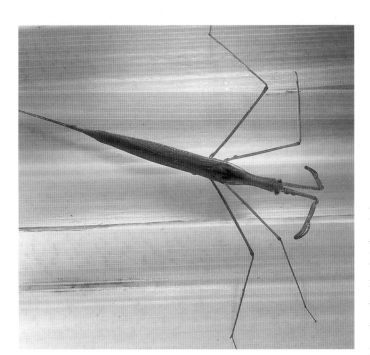

Assassin bug
(*Apiomerus*)

▲ WATER LOVERS

Water stick insects (*Ranatra linearis*) live in ponds and streams. They have long, slender legs and bodies, which camouflage them from enemies. On the insect's rear is a long, thin spine, which it uses as a breathing tube. The bug draws in air from above the surface, while the rest of its body remains submerged.

BLOOD-SUCKERS ▶

Assassin bugs are stealthy hunters that feed on other minibeasts. They sometimes look very similar to their prey so they can creep up stealthily. When the bug catches a victim, it sucks the juices from its body. Some assassin bugs live in dry places. This species comes from Arizona, USA.

▲ LIVING LANTERN

The lantern bug (*Fulgora*) is named for the pale tip on its snout. Although it looks like a tiny lantern, the tip does not give out light. This bug lives in the rainforests of south-east Asia. Another type of lantern bug has a huge false head, which looks like an alligator's snout.

Useful Bugs
Some types of bugs, including scale insects, are used by people. The bodies of cochineal scales can be crushed to extract cochineal, a red food dye. The Aztecs of Mexico used cochineal dye hundreds of years ago.

Body Parts

Garden chafer
(*Phyllopertha horticola*)

Head

Thorax

Abdomen

Human bodies are supported by a bony skeleton. Beetles, bugs and other insects have no inner skeleton. Instead, they are protected by a hard outer layer called an exoskeleton. This layer is waterproof and also helps to prevent the insect from drying out in hot weather. The exoskeleton is airtight, but it has special holes called spiracles that allow the insect to breathe.

The word 'insect' comes from a Latin word meaning 'in sections'. Like other insects, beetles' and bugs' bodies are made up of three main parts. All have a head, a thorax (middle section) and an abdomen (rear section). Almost all adult beetles and bugs have six legs, and most have two pairs of wings, which enable them to fly.

▲ THREE SECTIONS

A beetle's main sense organs, the antennae and eyes, are on its head. Its wings and legs are attached to the thorax. The abdomen contains the digestive and reproductive organs. When on the ground, the abdomen is covered by the beetle's wings.

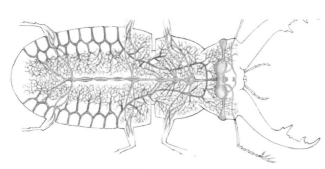

■ Respiratory system ■ Nervous system

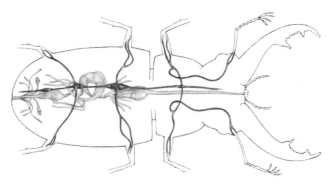

■ Digestive system ■ Circulatory system ■ Reproductive system

▲ BREATHING AND NERVOUS SYSTEMS

The respiratory (breathing) system has spiracles (openings) that lead to a network of tubes. The tubes allow air to reach all parts of the insect's body. The nervous system receives messages from the sense organs, and sends signals to the insect's muscles to make it move.

▲ OTHER BODY SYSTEMS

The digestive system breaks down and absorbs food. The circulatory system includes a long, thin heart that pumps blood through the body. The abdomen contains the reproductive parts. Males have two testes that produce sperm. Females have two ovaries that produce eggs.

◄ IN COLD BLOOD

Like all insects, beetles and bugs are cold-blooded animals. This means that the temperature of their body is similar to their surroundings. Insects control their body temperature by moving about. To warm up, beetles and bugs bask in the sun, as this leaf beetle (Chrysomelidae) is doing. If they need to cool their bodies, they move into the shade.

SURVIVING THE COLD ►

This tiger-beetle egg (*Cicindela*) is buried in the soil. In some parts of the world, winters are too cold for most adult insects to survive. The adult insects die, but their eggs, or young, can survive in the soil because it is warmer. When spring arrives, the young insects emerge, and so the species survives.

Rhinoceros beetle
(*Megasoma elephas*)

BEETLE CAR

During the 1940s, the tough, rounded beetle shape inspired the German car manufacturer Volkswagen to produce one of the world's most popular family cars, the VW Beetle. The car's tough outer shell, just like that of a beetle, helped it to achieve a good safety record. The design proved so successful that the Beetle car was recently improved and relaunched.

▲ MOVING FORTRESS

The rhinoceros beetle is very well armoured. Its tough exoskeleton covers and protects its whole body. The cuticle (outer skin) on its head forms three long points that look like a rhinoceros's horns. With all that armour, it is fairly safe for this beetle to move about!

On the Move

Beetles and bugs are expert movers. They can fly, run, leap and even swim. Some species are wingless, but most of those that have wings fly well. All adult beetles and bugs have six flexible, jointed legs, divided into four main sections. Many species have claws on their feet, which help them to cling on to smooth surfaces. Others have a flat pad between the claws, with hundreds of tiny hairs. The pads allow the insects to scramble up walls and even walk upside-down.

Squash bug
(Coreus marginatus)

▲ JOINTED LEGS

Like all beetles and bugs, squash bugs have four main sections in their legs. The top part is called the coxa, next comes the femur or upper leg, then the tibia or lower leg. The fourth section, the tarsus, is the part that touches the ground. You can also see the bug's feeding tube under its head.

▲ SPEEDY RUNNER

Tiger beetles (*Cicindela* species) are one of the fastest insects – they can cover up to 60cm a second. As it runs, the front and hind legs on one side of its body touch the ground at the same time as the middle leg on the other side. This steadies the beetle, like a three-legged stool.

◄ LONG LEAPER

Leafhopper bugs (Cicadellidae family) are long-jump champions! When preparing to leap, the bug gathers its legs beneath it like a runner on the starting block. Muscles that connect the upper and lower leg contract (shorten) to straighten the leg and fling the bug into the air.

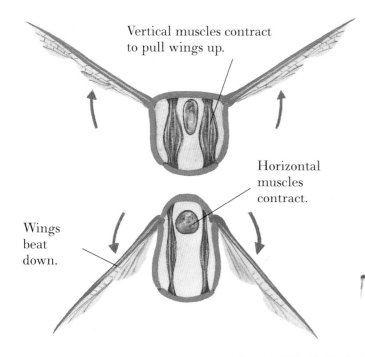

◄ SOIL SHIFTER

The burying, or sexton, beetle uses its strong front legs for digging. These ground-dwelling insects bury small animals (such as mice) in the ground to provide food for their young. The beetle's front legs are armed with little prongs that act as shovels, pushing the soil aside as it digs into the earth.

Burying beetle
(*Nicrophorus humator*)

ROWING THROUGH WATER ►

Great diving beetles (*Dytiscus marginalis*) are strong swimmers. Their flattened hind legs are covered with long-haired fringes, which act like broad paddles. The two back legs push together against the water, helping the insect to 'row' itself forward.

Vertical muscles contract to pull wings up.

Horizontal muscles contract.

Wings beat down.

◄ FLIGHT MUSCLES

Unlike flies, the beetle uses only its delicate rear wings for flying. Vertical muscles attached to the top and bottom of the thorax contract to flatten it. This makes the wings move up. Horizontal muscles along the body then contract to pull the thorax up, making the beetle's wings flip down. The action of the thorax controls the wings and propels the insect along.

Spotted longhorn
(*Strangalia maculata*)

GRACEFUL FLIER ►

A spotted longhorn beetle takes to the air. Like other insects, these beetles have two sets of flying muscles in their thorax (mid-body section). The hard front wings are held up to help steady the insect in flight. Most beetles are competent fliers, but they do not specialize in flying like some other insect species.

Focus on

1 When on the ground, the wing cases of the cockchafer beetle (*Melolontha melolontha*) meet over its body. The delicate rear wings are folded under the elytra and cannot be seen. Cockchafer beetles are also known as May bugs or June bugs, as it is in these months that they are usually seen.

Beetles, bugs and other insects are the only animals without a backbone that are able to fly. They take to the air to escape from their enemies and to move from place to place in search of food. Most beetles and bugs are expert fliers.

Bugs with two pairs of wings use both sets for flying. Their front and rear wings flap up and down together. The hardened front wings of a beetle are called elytra. They are not used for powering flight but steady the beetle as it flies. The long rear wings sweep up and down to power the beetle through the air.

2 A cardinal beetle (*Pyrochroa serraticornis*) prepares for take-off by raising its front wings out of the way and flexing its rear flight muscles. This process checks that the wings are in good working order and warms the beetle's muscles for the flight ahead. When the warm-up is finished, the beetle is ready to go.

3 A black-tipped soldier beetle (*Rhagonycha fulva*) positions itself for take-off like a plane taxiing down a runway. It finds a breezy spot by climbing a tall plant stem. Then it balances its body on top. In this exposed place, the wind may carry it away as it raises its wings. If not, the beetle will launch itself by leaping into the air.

Beetles in Flight

4 A cockchafer manoeuvres between plant stems. Its wing cases help to provide the lift it needs to remain airborne. Long rear wings provide flapping power to propel the beetle through the air. Cockchafers are clumsy fliers and sometimes stray into houses on dark evenings, drawn by the light. Indoors, the beetle may crash into objects in the unfamiliar setting, but it is so well armoured that it is rarely hurt.

5 A freeze-frame photograph shows the flapping wing movements of a *Pectocera fortunei* beetle in mid-flight. These small, light beetles find it fairly easy to stay airborne. However, their small size is a disadvantage in windy conditions, when they are sometimes blown off course.

6 A cockchafer prepares to land on an oak leaf. The beetle's rear wings are angled downwards to help it lose height. As it comes in to land, the legs will move forward to take the beetle's weight on the leaf. The veins that strengthen the delicate rear wings can be clearly seen in this picture.

Senses

Beetles and bugs have keen senses, but they do not sense the world in the same way that humans do. Most beetles and bugs have good eyesight and a keen sense of smell, but no sense of hearing. The main sense organs are on the head.

Most beetles and bugs have two large eyes, called compound eyes because they are made up of many tiny lenses. These are particularly good at sensing movement. Some beetles and bugs also have simple, bead-like eyes on top of their heads, which are sensitive to light and dark.

The antennae are the main sense tools for most beetles and bugs. They are used for smelling and feeling, and in some species for hearing and tasting, too. Antennae come in various shapes — some beetles and bugs have special feelers called palps on their mouthparts.

Sensitive hairs all over the insects' bodies pick up tiny currents in the air, which may alert them to enemies nearby.

◀ **SPINY SENSORS**
Tanner beetles (*Prionus coriarius*) have long, curving antennae. The antennae are covered with patterns of tiny hairs. Each hair is attached to a nerve that sends signals to the insect's brain when the hair is moved.

▲ **BRANCHING ANTENNAE**
This unusual beetle from Central America has branched antennae that look like the antlers of a stag. The branches are usually held closed, but the insect can also fan them out to pick up distant smells on the wind, such as the scent of a faraway mate. Smells such as these would be far too faint for humans to detect.

SMELL AND TOUCH ▶
Longhorn beetles (Cerambycidae) are named after their long antennae. An insect's antennae are sometimes called its 'feelers'.
The term is rather misleading — the antennae *are* used for feeling, but their main function is to pick up scents. Long antennae like the longhorn beetle's are especially sensitive to smell and touch.

◄ **ELBOW-SHAPED**
The weevil's antennae are found on its long nose. Many weevils have jointed antennae, which bend in the middle like a human arm at the elbow. Some have special organs at the base of their antennae, which vibrate to sound and act as ears. This brush-snouted weevil (*Rhina tarbirostris*) has a bushy 'beard' of long, sensitive hairs on its snout.

COMPOUND EYES ►
The huge eyes of the harlequin beetle (*Acrocinus longimanus*) cover its head. Only the area from which its antennae sprout remains uncovered. Each compound eye is made up of hundreds of tiny lenses. Scientists believe that the signals from each lens build up to create one large picture. Even so, scientists are not sure what beetles and bugs see.

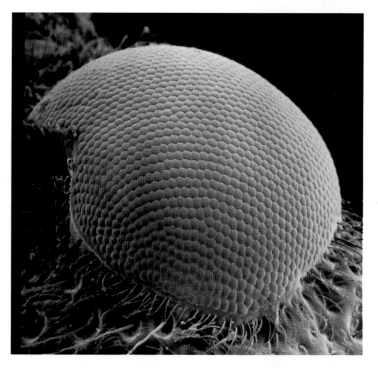

◄ **TINY LENSES**
A close-up of a beetle's compound eye shows that it is made up of many tiny facets, each of which points in a slightly different direction. Each is made up of a lens at the surface and a second lens inside. The lenses focus light down a central structure inside the eye, called the rhabdome, on to a bundle of nerve fibres, which are behind the eye. The nerve fibres then send messages to the brain. The hundreds of tiny lenses probably do not create the detailed, focused image produced by the human eye. However, they can pick up colours and shapes and are very good at detecting tiny movements.

Plant-eaters and Pests

Beetles and bugs do not always eat the same food throughout their lives. Larvae often eat very different foods from their parents. Some adult beetles and bugs do not feed at all, and instead put all their energy into finding a mate and reproducing very quickly.

Most bugs and some beetles are herbivores. Different species feed on the leaves, buds, seeds and roots of plants, on tree wood or on fungi. Many plant-eaters become pests when they feed on cultivated plants or crops. Other beetles and bugs are carnivores, or recycle waste by consuming dead plants or animals. Others nibble things that humans would not consider edible, such as clothes, woollen carpets, wooden furniture and even animal dung.

▲ TUNNEL-EATERS

This tree has been eaten by bark beetles (Scolytidae). Females lay their eggs under tree bark. When the young hatch, each eats its way through the wood to create a long, narrow tunnel just wide enough to squeeze through.

Squash bug
(Coreus marginatus)

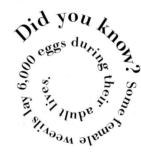

Did you know? Some female weevils lay 6,000 eggs during their adult lives.

◄ SQUASH-LOVERS

Squash bugs are named after their favourite food. The squash-plant family includes courgettes and pumpkins. This bug is about to nibble a courgette flower bud. Most squash bugs are green or brown in colour. They feed on the green parts of squash plants, and also on the seeds, which harms future crops. The insects are a pest in the USA.

▲ A PLAGUE OF APHIDS

Aphids are small, soft-bodied bugs. They use their sharp, beak-like mouths to pierce the stems of plants and suck out the sap inside. Aphids feed on the sap of plants, which is found in the stems and veins of leaves. These insects breed very quickly in warm weather.

▲ BEETLE ATTACK

Colorado beetles (*Leptinotarsa decemlineata*) are high on the list of dangerous insects in many countries. The beetles originally came from western USA, where they ate the leaves of local plants. When European settlers came and cultivated potatoes, the beetles ate the crop and did great damage. Colorado beetles later spread to become a major pest in Europe, but are now controlled by pesticides.

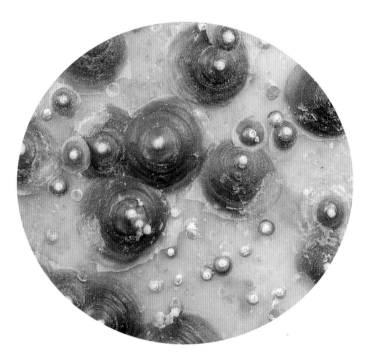

▲ SCALY FEEDERS

Most female scale insects (Coccoidae family) have neither legs nor wings, but they can be identified as bugs from the way their mouth is formed. Scale insects are usually well camouflaged, but the species shown here can be seen clearly. They are feeding on a juicy melon by piercing the skin and sucking up the sap.

▲ THE EVIL WEEVIL

These grains of wheat have been infested by grain weevils (*Sitophilus zeamais*). The adult weevils bore through the grain's hard case with their long snouts to reach the soft kernel inside. Females lay their eggs inside the kernels. Then, when the young hatch, they can feed in safety.

Scavengers and Hunters

Ground beetle
(*Lorica pilicornis*)

▲ **SPEEDY HUNTER**
A ground beetle feeds on a juicy worm it has caught. Ground beetles are a large family of beetles, with over 20,000 species. Many species cannot fly, hence their name. However, most ground beetles are fast runners. The beetle uses its speed to overtake its fleeing victim. Once trapped, the victim is firmly grabbed in the beetle's powerful jaws.

Many beetles and some bugs are carnivores (meat-eaters). Some hunt and kill live prey, others prefer their meat dead. Called scavengers, they feed on the remains of animals. Some other beetles and bugs are parasites that live on larger animals and eat their flesh, or drink their blood, without killing them.

Most predator beetles and bugs hunt fellow insects or other minibeasts such as millipedes. Some tackle larger game, such as fish, tadpoles, frogs, snails and worms. Beetles and bugs use a variety of different tricks and techniques to catch and overpower their prey. Most beetles seize their victims in their jaws, and crush or crunch them up to kill them. Bugs suck their victims' juices from their bodies while they are still alive.

◄ **GONE FISHING**
Great diving beetles (*Dytiscus marginalis*) are fierce aquatic hunters. They hunt down fish, tadpoles, newts and minibeasts that live in ponds and streams. This beetle has caught a stickleback. It grabs the fish in its jaws, then injects it with digestive juices that dissolve the fish's flesh. When the victim finally stops struggling and dies, the beetle begins to feed.

Famous Victim

Charles Darwin (1809–1882) was a British naturalist who first developed the theory of evolution – the idea that species develop over time to fit their environment.

Darwin's theory was inspired by a trip to South America to study wildlife. On returning to Britain, Darwin fell victim to a mysterious illness, which weakened him for the rest of his life. Some historians believe that he was bitten by a South American assassin bug that carried a dangerous disease.

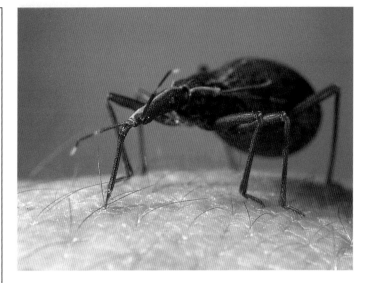

▲ VAMPIRE BEETLE

Most assassin bugs (Reduviidae family) are killers. Many species hunt minibeasts and suck their juices dry. Some are parasites. The species above feeds on humans by injecting their skin with a pain-killer so it can feast unnoticed.

EATEN ALIVE ▶

This shield bug *(Palomena prasina)* has caught a caterpillar. With a victim in its clutches, it uses its curving mouthparts to suck its prey dry. Most types of shield bugs are plant-eaters, but some hunt living creatures. The bugs use their front legs to hold their victims steady while they feast on them.

Did you know? *Great diving beetles store air under their wings when they dive.*

◀ NO ESCAPE

A snail-hunter beetle (*Calisoma*) tackles a small snail. To protect itself, the snail retreats into its shell and seals the opening with slime. In response, the beetle squirts a liquid into the shell to dissolve the slime and kill the snail.

Escaping Danger

The naturalist Charles Darwin's theory of evolution explains how only the fittest animals survive to breed and pass on their characteristics to the next generation. The key to survival is escaping danger. Beetles and bugs have many enemies in the natural world. They also have many ways of avoiding attack. Many species run, fly, hop or swim away, but some species are also armed with weapons. Some bugs and beetles can bite or use sharp spines for protection. Others are armed with poisonous fluids or taste nasty. These insects are often brightly coloured, which tells predators such as birds to stay away.

▲ **PROTECTIVE SPINES**
A weevil (*Lixus barbiger*) from the island of Madagascar has an impressive array of sharp spines on its back. Few predators will try such a prickly morsel – if they do, the pain may make them drop their meal!

▲ **READY TO SHOOT**
Desert skunk beetles (*Eleodes armata*) defend themselves by shooting a foul-smelling spray from their abdomens. This beetle has taken up a defensive posture by balancing on its head with its abdomen raised in the air. It is ready to fire its spray if an intruder comes close. Most predators will back away.

▼ **WHAT A STINK**
Squash bugs (*Coreus marginatus*) are also known as stink bugs because of the smelly spray they produce to ward off enemies. Like other insects, squash bugs do not actively *decide* to defend themselves. They instinctively react when their sense organs tell them that danger is near.

▼ TRICKY BEETLE

The devil's coach-horse beetle has several ways of defending itself from attack. First, it raises its tail in a pose that mimics a stinging scorpion (below). This defence is a trick, for the beetle cannot sting. If the trick does not work, the beetle gives off an unpleasant smell to send its enemies reeling. If all else fails, it delivers a painful bite with its large jaws.

Blistering Attack

The blister beetles (Meloidae family) *give off a chemical that causes human and animal skin to blister. Centuries ago, the chemical was thought to cure warts. Doctors applied blister beetles to the skin of patients suffering from the infection. The 'cure' was probably painful and did not work.*

Devil's coach-horse beetle
(Staphylinus olens)

◀ PLAYING DEAD

This weevil from East Africa is trying to fool an enemy by playing dead. It drops to the ground and lies on its back with its legs curled in a lifeless position. This defence works well on enemies that eat only live prey. However, it does not work on the many predators that are not fussy whether their victims are alive or dead.

WARNING COLOURS ▶

The cardinal beetle's body contains chemicals that have a terrible taste to predators. The beetle's blood-red colour helps to warn its enemies away. The colour coding will only work if the predator has tried to eat another beetle of the same species. If so, it will recognize the species by its colour and leave it alone.

Cardinal beetle
(Pyrochroa coccinea)

FOCUS on

Ladybirds are the only insects that many people will touch because they are known to be harmless. There are more than 4,000 different types of ladybirds in temperate and tropical countries all over the world. The insects are easy to recognize because of their rounded body shape. Most ladybirds are brightly coloured (red, yellow or orange) with black spots. These colours warn predators that ladybirds taste horrible.

Farmers and gardeners appreciate ladybirds because they are carnivores and feed on aphids and other minibeasts that cause damage to crops. One ladybird can eat up to 50 aphids a day. During the late 1800s, ladybirds were used to control the cottony cushion scale (*Icerya purchasi*) – a bug that threatened to destroy all the lemon trees in California, USA.

FLYING COLOURS

The eyed ladybird (*Anatis ocellata*) is a large European species. Most ladybirds are red with black spots. Some have yellow or white spots, or multi-coloured markings, like this species (above). Some ladybirds have stripes instead of spots, and others are black with no markings at all.

HEADS OR TAILS?

A seven-spot ladybird (*Coccinella septempunctata*) scurries across a leaf. Like all ladybirds, its bright colours are found on the elytra (wing cases), which fold over the insect's back. The head and thorax are black. The pale markings that look like eyes are actually on the thorax.

Ladybirds

FLY AWAY HOME

A ladybird in flight shows that, like other beetles, the insect holds its wing cases out of the way when flying. In spring, ladybirds lay their eggs on plants infested with aphids. When the hungry young ladybird grubs hatch, they devour large quantities of the plant-eating pests.

HEAVEN-SENT HELPERS

A ladybird munches an aphid. Ladybirds are popular with market gardeners because they eat aphids and other insects that attack trees and crops. In medieval times, Europeans believed that ladybirds were sent by the Virgin Mary to help farmers – hence the name ladybird.

WINTER SLEEP

Ladybirds cluster on a twig in winter. They survive the cold by entering a deep sleep called hibernation. They hibernate together in large numbers, in sheds, cellars or under tree bark. Collectors use this period to harvest large quantities of the beetles to sell to suppliers and garden shops for pest control.

Natural Disguises

Many beetles and bugs have colours and patterns on their bodies that disguise them in the natural world. Such disguises are called camouflage and hide the insects from their predators. Various species imitate natural objects, including sticks, grass, seeds, bark and thorns. Others are disguised as unpleasant objects, such as animal droppings, which predators avoid when looking for food.

Some beetles and bugs have another clever way of surviving — they mimic the colour or shape of insects such as wasps and ants that are poisonous or can sting. Predators recognize and avoid the warning signs of the harmless imitators, mistaking them for the dangerous minibeasts.

▲ BLADERUNNER

The top of this grass stem is actually a damsel bug (*Stenodema laengatum*) posing as a blade of grass. This bug's camouflage helps it to hide from its enemies — *and* sneak up on its prey, for the damsel bug is also a fierce predator.

Wasp beetle
(*Clytus arietis*)

▲ STRIPY WARNING

This beetle's bold black-and-yellow stripes suggest it is a wasp, armed with a painful sting. Although the insect is harmless, the warning colours are enough to put most predators off.

UNDER COVER ▶

A group of female scale insects (Coccoidae family) feed on a bay tree, disguised by their camouflage. The bugs also produce a nasty-tasting waxy white substance around their bodies. In this way, they can feed without being attacked by their enemies.

THORNY PROBLEM ▶

The sharp thorns on this twig look like part of the plant. They are, in fact, thorn bugs (*Umbonia crassicornus*). Each bug perfects its disguise by pointing in the same direction as the others on the twig. If they pointed in different directions, the bugs would look less like part of the plant. Even if a predator does spot the bugs, their prickly spines deter any passing enemy.

◀ ANT COSTUME

This treehopper (*Cyphonia clavata*) from the West Indies is a master of disguise. Its green body and transparent wings make it almost invisible when feeding upon leaves. In addition, it has an amazing black ant disguise on its back, which can be seen clearly by predators. True ants are armed with biting jaws and can also squirt stinging acid at their enemies. Predators will avoid them at all costs, and so the insect's clever disguise allows it to feed without being disturbed.

EYE SPY ▶

Click beetles have mottled colours that help them to blend in with grass or tree bark. The eyed click beetle (*Alaus oculatus*, right) has two large eyespots on its thorax. These resemble the eyes of a large predator, such as an owl. These frightening markings will be enough to stop any predatory bird from attacking the beetle.

Focus on

At nightfall in warm countries, the darkness may be lit up by hundreds of tiny green-yellow lights. The lights are produced by insects called fireflies, also known as glow-worms. There are over 1,000 different types of fireflies, but not all species glow in the dark. The light is produced by special organs in the insects' abdomens. Fireflies are nocturnal (night-active) beetles. Some species produce a continuous greenish glow, others flash their lights on and off. These signals are all designed for one purpose — to attract a mate.

FIREFLY ANATOMY
Fireflies are flat and slender. Most are dark brown or black, with orange or yellow markings. The light organs are found in their abdomens. Most species have two sets of wings, but in some, the females have no wings at all.

PRODUCING LIGHT
A male firefly flashes his light to females nearby. He produces light when chemicals mix in his abdomen, causing a reaction that releases energy in the form of light. In deep oceans, many sea creatures produce light in a similar way, including fish and squid.

CODED SIGNALS
A female firefly climbs on to a grass stem to signal with her glowing tail. Each species of firefly has its own sequence of flashes, which serves as a private mating code. On warm summer evenings, the wingless females send this code to the flashing males that fly above.

Fireflies

FALSE CODE

Most adult fireflies feed on flower nectar or do not eat at all. However, the female of this North American species is a meat-eater – and her prey is other fireflies. When the flightless female sees a male firefly of a different species circling overhead, she flashes his response code to attract him to the ground. When he lands nearby, she pounces and eats him. She also flashes to males of her own species to attract them to her for mating.

PULSE OF LIGHT

A group of fireflies light up a tree by a bridge as they signal to one another. In parts of Asia, some species of fireflies gather in large groups on trees. When one insect, called a pacemaker, flashes its light, all the other fireflies on the tree begin to flash their lights at the same time and to the same pattern. When this happens, the whole tree can be seen to glow and pulse with brilliant flashes of light.

YOUNG FIREFLIES

Like the adults, firefly larvae also make light. It is only the young, wingless insects and the flightless females that are called glow-worms. Young fireflies hatch from eggs laid in moist places by the females. Unlike most of their parents, all firefly larvae are meat-eaters. They kill slugs and snails by injecting them with poison. The young insects use their sharp jaws to hook the snails out of their shells and then gobble them up.

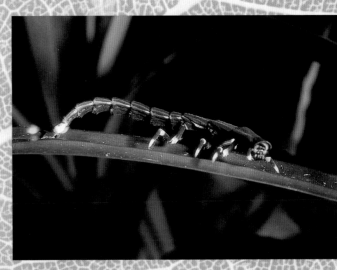

Attracting a Mate

One of the most important tasks for any animal is to continue its species by breeding. Beetles and bugs are no exception, and most must mate before they produce young.

Many beetles and bugs use scent to attract the opposite sex. They give off special smells that can travel a long distance through the air. The opposite sex then follow the trail of scent to find a partner to mate with. Some species use sound to attract a mate that is far away.

At close quarters, beetles and bugs may partly identify one another by sight. If two or more males are attracted to one female, the rivals may fight for the chance to mate. In some species, males and females spend several hours courting — checking that they have found a suitable mate. In other species, mating takes only a few minutes, after which the two insects go their separate ways.

▲ **IRRESISTIBLE SMELL**
Bark beetles (Scolytidae) live in tree trunks. Females of some species produce a scent, which male beetles pick up using their antennae. Sometimes, many males are drawn to just one female.

Did you know? Most beetles mate for only a few seconds but some mate for hours.

Rhododendron leafhopper
(Graphocephala fennahi)

◄ **SOUND SIGNALS**
Male leafhopper bugs 'sing' to attract their partners. They produce little squeaks and rasping sounds by rubbing their wings against their abdomen. The female insects have special hearing organs that can detect the high-pitched calls made by their mates. The sounds are far too quiet for humans to hear.

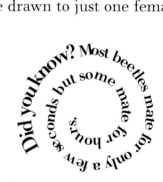

Ominous Sound

Deathwatch beetles (Xestobium rufovillosum)
live in rotting logs and also in wooden
buildings. During the breeding season, they tap
on the wood at night to attract a mate. These
sounds, sometimes heard by sick people awake
at night, were once thought to be very unlucky.
The tapping was believed to be an omen of
death – hence the beetle's name.

▲ SPOTTING A MATE

Seven-spot ladybirds (*Coccinella septempunctata*)
mate on a leaf. The male mounts the female
to release sperm to fertilize her eggs. Ladybirds
use sight to identify one another. They are
guided to their own species by the different
numbers of spots on their elytra (wing cases).
Once they have found one of their own kind,
they can mate successfully to produce young.

◄ FROG LEGS

This athletic-
looking insect is a
Malayan frog beetle.
The species owes its
name to the male
beetle's
powerful,
frog-like hind
legs. The insect uses
his legs for leaping,
but also for breeding.
He clings on to the
female beetle
during mating,
which helps to make
sure that the union
is fertile.

Malayan frog beetle
(Sagra buqueti)

▲ MALE AND FEMALE

A male aphid mates with a female. Many male
and female beetles and bugs look similar to one
another, but some aphids are different. The
females have plump, green bodies. The males
are thinner, with dark bodies and large wings.
There are more female aphids than males.
Males appear only in autumn, to mate with the
females. The females lay fertilized eggs, which
survive the winter and hatch in spring.

Focus on Stag

Courtship is a risky business for some types of beetles. Males will fight to mate with a female – sometimes to the death. Stag beetles (*Lucanus cervus*) are fighting beetles. They owe their name to the huge jaws of the male, which resemble a stag's antlers. The female stag beetle releases a scent which attracts males to her. Males can sense this scent from up to 1km away. If two rival males appear, they may fight. Each beetle tries to hoist his rival in the air and smash him to the ground.

1 A male stag beetle displays his fearsome horns, which can be as long as his body. The beetle uses its jaws not for feeding, but to frighten away rival males and predators.

2 Like the male stag beetle, the body of the female is well armoured. Her jaws are much smaller than the male's, however, and are not designed for fighting. The female's main purpose is to survive long enough to breed.

3 Two male beetles size each other up on the prime breeding ground of an old tree stump. Each male tries to frighten the other with his giant horns. If neither beetle backs down and scuttles away, the fight will start.

Beetle Contests

4 The rival males begin to wrestle. As they lock horns, each tries to gain the upper hand by gripping his enemy. The fierce-looking jaws rarely do serious damage, but the fight tests the strength and endurance of both insects.

5 The strongest beetle grips his enemy in his jaws and lifts him high. The other beetle is helpless in this position, but the victor struggles to keep his balance. One slip and the other beetle could take control.

6 The victorious beetle ends the contest by dashing his rival to the ground, or by throwing him off the log. If the loser lands on his back, he may be unable to get up – particularly if he is wounded. The defeated beetle may well be eaten alive by predatory insects, such as ants. The strongest male wins his right to mate with the female, and so pass on his characteristics to the next generation. This process ensures that only the strongest genes are passed on, guaranteeing the survival of the fittest.

The Life Cycle of Beetles

▲ **LAYING EGGS**
A female cardinal beetle (*Pyrochroa coccinea*) lays its eggs in dead wood. The hard tip of the beetle's abdomen pierces the wood to lay the eggs inside. When the eggs hatch, the log provides the larvae with a hiding place from predators. They feast on the timber until they are fully grown.

Beetles and bugs have different life cycles. During their lives, beetles pass through four stages. From eggs, they hatch into larvae (young) called grubs. The grubs do not look like their parents. Some have legs, but many look like long, pale worms. They all live in different places from the adults and eat different food.

Beetle larvae are hungry feeders. They feed, grow and moult their skins several times, but do not change form or grow wings. When the larva is fully grown, it develops a hard case and enters a resting stage, called a pupa. Inside the case, the grub's body is totally dissolved and then rebuilt. It emerges from its pupa as a winged adult. This amazing process is called complete metamorphosis. The word 'metamorphosis' means transformation.

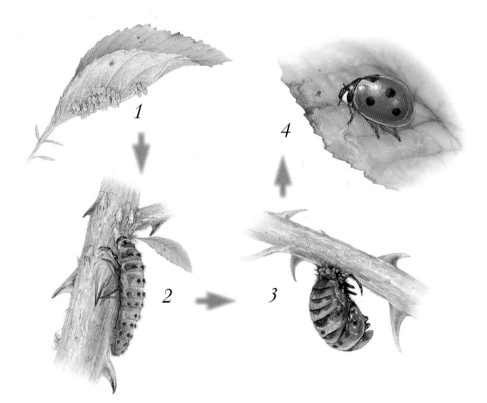

◄ **THE FOUR STAGES**
There are four stages in a beetle's life cycle. It begins life as an egg (1), then becomes a larva or grub (2). The full-grown larva then becomes a pupa (3) before it reaches adulthood (4). At each stage, the beetle's appearance is almost totally different from the last stage. In a way, a developing beetle is several animals in one. When the beetle finally emerges from its pupa as an adult, it is ready to breed, and so the life cycle can begin again.

◄ BEETLE EGGS

The female ladybird glues her eggs on to leaves so that they stand on end. Beetle eggs are generally rounded or oval. They are usually yellow, green or black for camouflage. Most eggs are laid in spring or summer, and most hatch between one week and one month later. Some eggs are laid in autumn and hatch the following spring. They take longer to hatch because of the cooler conditions.

LARVA ►

This cockchafer larva (*Melolontha melolontha*) looks nothing like the adult. Its long, fat body is very different from the adult's rounded shape. However, unlike many beetle grubs, it does have legs. The larva has no compound eyes or long antennae. Nor does it have wings, but moves about by wriggling its way through the soil.

◄ PUPA

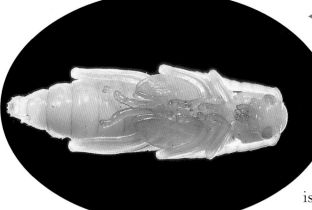

When a beetle grub is fully grown, it attaches itself to a plant stem or hides underground. Then it develops a hard outer case to become a pupa. Unlike the grub, the pupa doesn't feed or move much. It looks dead, but inside its hard case, an amazing change is taking place. The insect's body breaks down into a kind of soup, and is reshaped into an adult beetle.

ADULT FORM ►

An adult seven-spot ladybird (*Coccinella septempunctata*) struggles out of its pupa case. It emerges complete with long, jointed legs, wings and antennae. Its yellow wing cases will develop spots after just a few hours. Some beetles spend only a week as pupae before emerging as fully grown adults. Others pass the whole winter in the resting stage, waiting to emerge until the following spring.

101

The Life Cycle of Bugs

Bugs develop in a different way from beetles. Most bugs hatch from eggs laid by females after mating. Newly hatched bugs are called nymphs and look like tiny adults, but they are wingless. Nymphs often eat the same food and live in the same places as their parents.

Unlike human skin, an insect's exoskeleton is not stretchy. Nymphs are hungry eaters, and as they feed and grow, their hard skins become too tight and must be shed several times. This process is called moulting. The nymphs then develop new skins, inside which there is space to grow. As they grow, they gradually sprout wings. After a final moult, the bugs emerge as winged adults. This process is called incomplete metamorphosis because, unlike beetles, bugs do not go through the pupa stage and totally rebuild their bodies.

▲ BUG EGGS
Like other young insects, most bugs start out as eggs. These little yellow balls are shield bug eggs (*Eysarcoris fabricii*). They are all at various stages of development. The yellow eggs on the left are more developed than the paler eggs on the right, and will soon hatch into young.

Did you know? In summer, female aphids give birth to up to 50 young in a week.

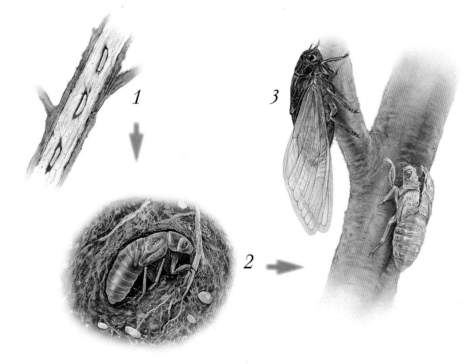

1

2

3

◀ THE THREE STAGES
There are three different stages in a bug's life. The first stage is the egg (1), from which the bug hatches as a nymph (2). The nymph gradually grows and moults a number of times. At each moult it becomes more like an adult. The wing buds appear after several moults, and gradually lengthen as the nymph reaches adulthood (3).

EASY TARGET ▶

This young shield bug looks like its parents, but it is wingless and cannot fly. After moulting, the nymph has no hard skin to protect it and is extremely vulnerable. At this stage, young bugs are 'sitting ducks,' and many fall victim to predators such as lizards and birds. After moulting, the new exoskeleton hardens within just a few hours. With luck, this new layer will protect the young bug for long enough to reach adulthood.

◀ FOAMY HIDEOUT

Some nymphs have special ways of avoiding predators. This froghopper nymph (*Philaemus spumarius*) hides inside the unpleasant-looking foam behind it, known as 'cuckoo spit'. The bug produces the froth itself by giving off a sticky liquid, which it blows into a foam. The cuckoo spit makes a good hiding place from predators, and also screens the bug from the sun.

YOUNG HUNTER ▶

Just a few hours after hatching, a young pond skater (*Gerris najas*, right) begins to live and feed on the water's surface, just like its parents. A pond skater's feet are covered in dense water-repellent hair, which allows it to walk on the surface of the water. Pond skaters are expert predators, catching other water creatures and then feeding by sucking out the victims' juices with their long feeding tubes.

◀ BREEDING WITHOUT MALES

In autumn, male and female aphids breed and lay eggs in the normal way. In summer, however, female aphids can reproduce without males, and give birth to live offspring without mating or even laying eggs. This aphid (left) is giving birth to a fully formed young. This amazing process is called parthenogenesis (meaning virgin birth.) The babies grow up quickly, and can themselves breed after just one week.

▲ SOIL DWELLERS

Click beetle larvae (Elateridae family) are called wireworms. They have worm-like bodies and tiny legs. Most are bright yellow or orange. Wireworms live in soil and feed on the roots of grasses. They can cause damage to crops by eating their roots.

▲ LIVELY LARVA

A ladybird larva (*Coccinella septempunctata*) munches aphids. Many grubs are legless or not quick on their feet, but young ladybirds are nimble and lively, like tiny lizards.

UNDER DUNG ▶

Beetles that live above ground need to find some way to protect themselves from enemies. This green tortoise beetle larva (*Cassida viridis*) is hiding from predators by carrying a lump of dung on its tail.

Young Beetles

The main purpose of an adult beetle is to reproduce. The goal for a larva is to reach adulthood, which it does by feeding, growing and avoiding predators. Most beetles lay their eggs on or near a suitable food source for their young, such as dead wood, plants or even in a living animal.

Various species of beetles spend different amounts of time as eggs, larvae, pupae and adults. Ladybirds spend just one week as an egg, three to six weeks as larvae and then another week as pupae. Stag beetles take longer to grow. They hatch after two weeks as an egg, but then spend up to five years as grubs living in dead wood and another eight months as pupae. Adult stag beetles live only a few months before they die.

▲ WOODBORERS

Metallic woodboring beetles (*Buprestidae* family) live in tunnels in dead wood. The larvae feed on the timber, but it is not very nourishing. So the young grubs must spend many years feeding before they are ready to pupate and become adults. One type of woodboring beetle spends 40 years in the timber before it is fully grown.

Deadly Beetle

The pupae of a particular kind of South African leaf beetle produce a deadly poison. Just the smallest trace of the poison can kill a large animal, such as a gazelle. Kalahari bushmen tip the points of their arrows with the beetle's poison before going on hunting trips. Preparing their weapons is very dangerous. The hunters take great care to make sure that the poison does not get into cuts or grazes on their own skin. If it does, they could die.

▲ HIDDEN TRAP

The tiger beetle larva (*Cicindela* species) is a stealthy predator. It makes a burrow in the soil and fills the entrance with its huge jaws. It then waits until a passing insect comes close enough to grab. The beetle's jaws snap shut and it drags its prey into its burrow to finish it off.

FREE AT LAST ▶

A nut weevil larva (*Curculio nucum*) pokes its head out of a hazel nut. Its mother drilled into the nut to lay her egg inside. The grub hatched and fed inside the nut, then gnawed its way to freedom. It will not spend long in the open air. Instead, it will quickly burrow into the soil, where it will pupate.

Caring for the Young

Oak roller weevil
(*Attelebus nitens*)

Most beetles and bugs do not actively care for their offspring. They simply lay their eggs on a suitable food source, and then leave the young to fend for themselves. A few species, though, are caring parents. Some beetles, such as oak roller weevils, take great effort to protect their eggs. Other species, such as burying beetles, feed their larvae themselves.

Cross-winged bugs, such as shield bugs, guard and watch over their nymphs until the babies become big enough to look after themselves. Passalid beetles take even greater care of their young. Like ants, termites, and some bees and wasps, they are social insects. Social insects live and work together in a group. These beetle parents, and even their older offspring, take great pains to rear their young.

Did you know? Some water beetles weave a web around the eggs to keep them dry.

▲ SAFE HOME

Oak roller weevils lay their eggs high up in oak trees. The females use their jaws to snip the oak leaves into sections. They then curl the leaves into tight rolls, in which they lay their eggs. Inside the rolls, the eggs are safe from predators that might eat the eggs or feed them to their own young.

CARING MUM ▶

A female shield bug, known as the parent bug (*Elasmucha grisea*), protects her young from a predatory spider. Her large brood of nymphs cluster behind her for safety. A distant relative, the male giant water bug, protects his eggs by carrying them on his body until they hatch.

106

Sacred Scarabs

Scarab beetles were sacred to the ancient Egyptians. They symbolized the sun-god, Ra. Each day, Ra rolled the fiery ball of the sun across the sky, just as the scarab beetle rolls a ball of dung to a suitable place to lay its eggs. The scarab beetle was a symbol of rebirth, and it was used to decorate tombs and many sacred objects.

◄ DUNG-ROLLERS

Dung beetles are part of the scarab beetle family (Scarabaeidae). These beetles and their young feed on the droppings of mammals such as buffalo. To provide for the young, the male and female beetles shape the dung into a ball. They then roll it to a safe place, where they bury it. The female beetle lays her eggs in the dung ball. When the young hatch, they will have a ready food supply in a safe hiding hole. The buried dung also helps to fertilize the soil.

▲ FAMILY GROUPS

Passalid beetles live in families. They inhabit rotting tree trunks, in a maze of tunnels. These parent beetles are tending pupae in their white cocoons. When the pupae emerge as adults, they stay in the nest to help rear the next generation of young.

▲ PERSONAL CARE

A burying beetle (*Nicrophorus humator*) crawls over a dead shrew. The parent beetles tunnel under the dead body to bury it. The female then lays her eggs on the animal. Some beetles wait for the young to hatch, then feed them the meat of the dead mammal themselves.

Homes and Habitats

Around the world, beetles and bugs are found in all sorts of different habitats. Most live in hot, tropical regions or in mild, temperate areas. Many beetles and bugs are found in places that have moderate or heavy rainfall, but some tough species manage to live in deserts. Others can survive on snow-capped mountains or frozen icefields, in caves, sewers and even hot springs.

Beetles and bugs that live in very cold or very hot places must be able to cope with extreme temperatures. Many survive the harsh weather as pupae, or as eggs in the soil. In deserts, most species are active at night, when the air is cooler. The toughest species can go for long periods without food or even water. These insects are small enough to shelter from storms or predators in tiny nooks and crannies.

▲ PARASITES
Bedbugs (*Cimex lectularius*) are parasites that live and feed on warm-blooded animals. Some species suck human blood. Bedbugs that infest birds and furry mammals live in their nests, or among their feathers or hair. Kept warm by their host animal, some bedbugs can even survive in cold places such as the Arctic.

Did you know? Water boatmen can fly many kilometres to find a new home.

◄ UPSIDE-DOWN WORLD
Water boatmen (*Notonecta maculata*) live upside-down in water. The bug hangs just below the water surface, and uses its oar-like legs to move about, rather like rowing. Like many bugs that live in water, the boatman is a hunter. It grabs minibeasts that have fallen into the water, and sucks their juices dry.

LONG LIMBS ▶

This stilt-legged bug (*Berytidae* family) lives in caves in the Caribbean. Its long, thin legs and antennae help it to feel its way in the dark. The legs and antennae are also covered with hairs that can detect the slightest air currents, alerting the bug to the presence of other animals.

◀ DESERT SURVIVOR

The fog-basking beetle (*Onymachris unguicularis*) lives in the Namib Desert, in southern Africa. This beetle has an ingenious way of drinking. When fog and mist swirl over the dunes, it does a handstand and points its abdomen in the air. Moisture gathers on its body, then trickles down special grooves on its back into its waiting mouth.

SURVIVING IN CAVES ▶

This beetle (*Aphaenops* species) lives in caves high in the Pyrenees Mountains, between France and Spain. Its body is not well camouflaged, but in the dark of the caves, disguise is not important. Scientists believe some cave-dwelling species developed from beetles that first lived in the caves during the last Ice Age, about a million years ago.

◀ DUNE DWELLER

The dune beetle (*Onymacris bocolor*) lives in the deserts of southern Africa. It is one of the few white beetles. White reflects the rays of the sun and helps to keep the insect cool. The pale colour also blends in well with the sand where it lives, which helps it to hide from predators. The beetle's elytra (wing cases) are hard and close-fitting, and so help to conserve (keep) precious body moisture in this dry region. Long legs raise the beetle's body above the burning desert sand.

109

Tropical Beetles and Bugs

An amazing range of beetles and bugs live in tropical countries, where the weather is always hot. In this climate, these cold-blooded insects can stay active all year round. Parts of the tropics have dense rainforests and this wealth of plant food means that rainforests contain more types of beetles and bugs than any other habitat on Earth. A single rainforest tree may hold several thousand different kinds of insects. Some beetles and bugs live high in the treetops. Others live among the tangled vegetation halfway up tall trees, or among the decaying plants and fungi of the forest floor.

The tropical regions are home to many brightly coloured beetles and bugs. Other species wear subtle colours that blend in with their home.

▲ BRIGHT BUG

Tropical shield bugs (Heteroptera order) come in many bright colours. Some are warning colours, which tell predators that these insects can defend themselves. This shield bug nymph from Indonesian can also produce a foul smell if attacked.

Did you know? Cicadas that live in moist places coat their bodies with a waterproof wax.

◄ UNDER COVER

Most jewel beetles and bugs are known for their bright, rainbow colours, but this species (Buprestidae family) from southern Africa is more subtly coloured. The hairs on the beetle's thorax add to its disguise, and may help repel attackers. Its bright, shiny relatives are often prized by collectors. Sometimes these unfortunate bugs are actually made into jewellery.

◀ BEAUTIFUL BEETLE

Tropical rainforests are home to some of the world's most spectacular beetles. Few are more splendid than this golden beetle from Central America. Surprisingly, the beetle's shiny colours work as camouflage. The insect looks like a raindrop glinting in the sun, so its enemies don't notice it. The colours are created when sunlight bounces off the insect's skin.

LURKING HUNTER ▶

This colourful assassin bug (Reduviidae) is from Africa. Like most of its family, it lies in wait for minibeasts, then sucks its victims dry. The bug can be seen clearly on a dark leaf, but it is well camouflaged in the tropical flowers and stems among which it hides. The eyespots on its back scare away enemies.

◀ CLOWN BUG

A harlequin bug from southern Africa rests on a tree seed. These bugs are named after clowns called harlequins, who wear costumes with bright patterns. In Australia, male, female and young harlequins are all different brilliant colours — red, yellow or blue with green spots. Some harlequin species make their homes high in the treetops.

BARK MIMIC ▶

A longhorn beetle (Cerambycidae family) from south-west Africa demonstrates the power of camouflage. The beetle's feelers and its square shape resemble the cracks and flaking texture of the tree bark, making it almost invisible. Its long antennae are spread wide to pick up scents in the wind.

Focus on

Cicadas are sometimes called locusts or harvest flies, but they are neither. These insects are bugs that live in the tropics and warm countries. They are well known for their noisy 'songs', which the males produce to attract a mate.

Like other bugs, cicadas undergo incomplete metamorphosis to become adults. Some species live longer than most other insects – periodical cicadas can be 17 years old before they reach adulthood. The bugs survive beneath the ground by gnawing on plant roots.

BIG BUG
Most cicadas are large insects and can be more than 4cm long. This giant cicada from Africa is even bigger and has a wingspan of 15cm.

RED EYE
This cicada from Australia is sucking plant sap. Its long, straw-like mouthparts pierce the plant stem. It has large red eyes – hence its name, red-eye cicada (*Psaltodea moerens*).

SINGING FOR A MATE
Male cicadas sing 'courtship songs' to attract the females. When the male flexes muscles in his abdomen, two thin, drum-like sheets of skin on the sides of the abdomen vibrate to make a stream of clicking sounds.

Cicadas

LAYING EGGS

After mating, the female cicada lays her eggs on a twig. She uses the sharp tip of the egg-layer on her abdomen to cut slits in the bark for hundreds of tiny eggs. The nymphs hatch about six weeks later. They drop to the ground and burrow into the soil to develop.

FINAL MOULT

When the cicada nymph is fully grown, it climbs out of the soil and clambers up a tree trunk for its final moult. This is an amazing sight. The back of the cicada's old skin bursts apart, and the young adult slowly struggles out. This bug is a dog-day cicada (*Canicularis* species), a species from North America. While it does not live quite as long as the periodical cicada, this nymph spends up to seven years underground before becoming an adult.

SPREAD YOUR WINGS

As the dog-day cicada scrambles clear of its old skin, its wings uncurl and lengthen. The bug spreads its wings out to dry. Until it can fly, it is an easy target for birds and lizards. The young adults fly off to sing for a few weeks before they die. During their brief adult lives, they will mate and lay eggs, so that a new generation of bugs will emerge from the soil.

Temperate Beetles and Bugs

The world's temperate regions lie north and south of the tropics. Temperate lands have a mild climate, with warm summers and cold winters. When trees and plants lose their leaves in winter, food is scarce for beetles and bugs, and many adult insects die. Their eggs or pupae survive to hatch in the spring. The natural vegetation of temperate regions is grassland or woodland. These rich food sources ensure that temperate lands are home to thousands of beetle and bug species.

Green shield bug
(Palomena prasina)

▲ SPITTING BLOOD

Bloody-nosed beetles (*Timarcha tenebricosa*) are large, slow-moving insects. Their striking black colour can attract unwelcome attention. To protect itself, this beetle has a secret weapon — it can spurt a bright red liquid from its mouth. Most predators will leave the beetle alone if faced with this frightening sight.

▲ COLOUR CHANGER

This shield bug lives on trees and shrubs. In the spring and summer it is bright green, but in autumn it turns reddish brown, like the leaves it lives on. The shield bug hibernates during the winter. When it re-emerges in the spring, its bright green colour will have returned. There are a number of types of shield bug. The gorse shield bug (*Piezodorus lituratus*) is red only as a young adult. After hibernation, it becomes yellow-green.

Hairy click beetle
(Athous hirtus)

◀ CLEVER CLICK

Click beetles get their name from the clicking sound they make. The beetle hooks its thorax together by locking a peg into a hole on its belly. When the peg is released with a click, it throws the beetle into the air, helping it to escape from enemies. The beetle also uses the click mechanism to right itself if it falls on its back.

WILD ROVER ▶

Rove beetles (Staphylinidae family) are a large beetle family, with more than 20,000 species. They are found in tropical and temperate lands worldwide. With their long, slim bodies, some species look like earwigs. Others are very hairy. Most species lurk under stones or in the soil.

Rove beetle
(Creophilus maxillosus)

◀ INSECT PARTNERS

Aphids produce a sweet liquid called honeydew – a favourite food of many ants. These ants are collecting honeydew from aphids on a foxglove. Some types of ants keep aphids in the same way that people keep cattle. They 'milk' the aphids by stroking them with their antennae. This makes the aphids release their honeydew. In return, the ants protect the aphids from ladybirds, and sting the aphids' enemies if they attack.

CANNIBAL CARDINALS ▶

The cardinal beetle is recognizable by its distinctive, bright red elytra (wing cases). Adults are usually found on flowering shrubs or tree trunks. The females lay their eggs under the dry bark of trees. When the eggs grow into larvae, they eat other insects that live in the tree. If the larvae cannot find food, they feed upon each other.

Cardinal beetle
(Pyrochroa coccinea)

115

Focus on Living

Some beetles and bugs live in and on fresh water – not only ponds and rivers but also icy lakes, mountain streams, muddy pools and stagnant marshes. Most of the larvae live in the water, where rich stocks of food make good nurseries.

Different types of beetles and bugs live at different depths in the water. Some live on the water surface or just below it. Other species swim in the mid-depths, or lurk in the mud or sand at the bottom. Beetles and bugs that live underwater carry a supply of air down with them so that they can breathe.

SURFACE SPINNERS

Whirligig beetles (*Gyrinus natator*) are oval, flattened beetles that live on the surface of ponds and streams. Their compound eyes are divided into two halves, designed to see above and below the water. When swimming, they move in circles, like spinning toys called whirligigs.

SKATING ON WATER

Pond skaters (*Gerris lacustris*) live on the water's surface. They move about like ice skaters, buoyed up by their light bodies. The bugs' legs make dimples on the surface of the water, but do not break it. When these bugs sense a drowning insect nearby, they skate over in gangs to feed on it.

SPINY STRAW

Water scorpions have long spines on their abdomens like true scorpions. The spines have no sting, but are used to suck air from the surface. Sensors on the spine tell the bug when it is too deep to breathe.

in Water

THE SCORPION STRIKES

Water scorpions (*Nepa cinerea*) are fierce predators. This bug has seized a stickleback fish in its pincer-like front legs. It then uses its mouthparts to pierce the fish's skin and suck its juices dry. Compared to some aquatic insects, water scorpions are not strong swimmers. They sometimes move about underwater by walking along water plants.

AIR SUPPLY

Saucer bugs (*Ilyacoris*) are expert divers. In order to breathe, the bug takes in air through spiracles (holes) in its body. Tiny bubbles of air are also trapped between the bug's body hairs, giving it its silvery colour. Saucer bugs use their front legs to grab their prey. They cannot fly, but move from pond to pond by crawling through the grass.

DIVING DOWN

You can often see water boatmen (*Corixa punctata*) just below the water surface, but they can also dive below. They use their back legs to row underwater, and breathe air trapped under their wings. The females lay their eggs on water plants or glue them to stones on the stream bed. The eggs hatch two months later.

Other Insects

Many species of insects are thought of as beetles or bugs. They may look similar or have similar habits, but scientists think they are different enough to put them in a separate order. For example, true flies (Diptera) go through a complete metamorphosis, just like beetles. However, they only have one pair of wings, instead of two.

Over the next few pages we look at some of the other orders of insects and investigate the characteristics that make them unique.

There are some features that all insects share. All insects have a head, a thorax and an abdomen, and three pairs of legs. They have antennae and compound eyes. Almost all insects hatch from eggs.

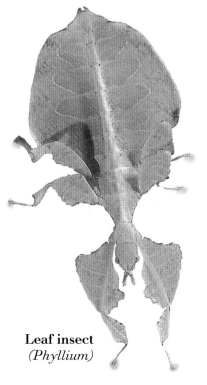

Leaf insect
(Phyllium)

▲ STICK AND LEAF INSECTS

Leaf insects resemble leaves or bark. Stick insects, which belong to the same order, look like twigs with their long, thin legs and bodies.

INSECT ORDERS ▶

This illustration shows 20 of the major insect orders, with each order represented by a particular insect. Some scientists have identified less than 25 orders, some more than 30. Some orders contain several familiar insects.

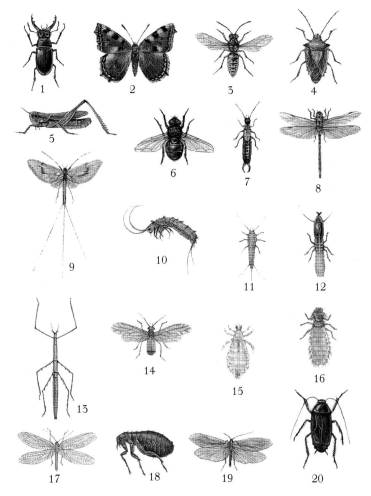

1. Coleoptera: beetle
2. Lepidoptera: butterfly
3. Hymenoptera: wasp
4. Hemiptera: shield bug
5. Orthoptera: grasshopper
6. Diptera: fly
7. Dermaptera: earwig
8. Odonata: dragonfly
9. Ephemeroptera: mayfly
10. Collembola: springtail

11. Thysanura: silverfish
12. Isoptera: termite
13. Phasmida: stick insect
14. Psocoptera: bark lice
15. Anoplura: sucking lice
16. Mallophaga: biting lice
17. Neuroptera: lacewing
18. Siphonaptera: flea
19. Trichoptera: caddisfly
20. Dictyoptera: cockroach

◄ CADDISFLIES

This strange creature is a caddisfly larva. It belongs to the Trichoptera order, which means 'hair wings'. The adults have two pairs of hairy, flimsy wings and look similar to moths. Their larvae grow up in ponds and streams, protected by silk cocoons and camouflaged with sticks and stones. The caddisfly larva undergoes a complete metamorphosis to become an adult.

COCKROACHES ►

Cockroaches belong to the order Dictyoptera, which means 'net wings'. They live in forests, caves and people's homes. Cockroaches hide by day and come out at night to feed. Once inside a house, it can be difficult to get rid of them.

Did you know? Some female earwigs lick their eggs to keep them free of infection.

Earwig
(Forficula auriculariam)

◄ EARWIGS

The Dermaptera order, which means 'skin wings', includes earwigs (left). These insects' abdomens end in a pair of long, fierce pincers. Their young hatch as nymphs. Insects in the Dermaptera order have slim, brown bodies and two pairs of wings. Their long rear wings are usually folded under their short, leathery, skin-like front wings, which have earned them their name.

LICE ►

Lice are parasitic insects that live on birds and mammals. They make up several orders, including biting (Mallophaga) and sucking (Anoplura) lice. All are wingless. Head lice, shown here, are sucking lice. They live and lay their eggs, called nits, in human hair.

True Flies

After beetles, flies are one of the largest insect orders. Over 90,000 different kinds of fly have been identified, including gnats, midges and mosquitoes. These hardy insects live almost everywhere on Earth, including the icy polar regions. Unlike beetles and bugs, flies have only one pair of wings. This is reflected in their order name, Diptera, which means 'two wings'. All that remains of the fly's hind wings are two little organs called halteres. These help the fly to balance and steer as it flies.

Ever unpopular, flies are considered dirty and carry diseases that can infect our food. Flies do have their uses, however. They fertilize flowers, and feed on dung and dead animals, reducing this waste around the world.

▲ FLY FOOD

This house fly is feeding on a piece of jelly. Taste sensors on its feet help it to detect its food. Like many kinds of flies, houseflies have mouths that work like sponges. They suck, or lick up, liquid foods such as sap and fruit juice. Some flies even feed on dung, rotting meat or blood.

Did you know? Over 10,000 species of craneflies are known to exist worldwide.

House fly
(Musca domestica)

INSECT ACROBATS ▶

This house fly is walking upside-down across the ceiling. Many flies have hooks and sticky pads on their feet, which help them to grip smooth surfaces. Their halteres (balancing organs) make them acrobatic fliers. They can hover, fly backwards and even land upside-down. Such skills help them to dodge fly-swatters.

▲ THIN AND FAT

Flies come in different shapes and sizes. Crane flies (Tipulidae family) such as the one above, are slim and delicate. Bluebottles and house flies are stout and chunky. Some flies are 0.5mm long – tinier than a pinhead. Others can measure a hundred times that size.

The Fly

This picture is taken from the horror film
The Fly. *In the film, a scientist turns into a fly after an experiment goes wrong. Gruesome special effects make the film particularly scary. The theme proved so popular with audiences that several different versions have been made.*

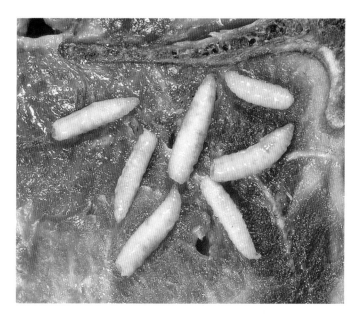

▲ FOUR-STEP LIVES

Young flies are known as maggots. Like beetles, flies have four stages in their life cycle. They begin life as eggs, laid by the females in water, rotting plants or meat, or on animals. The eggs hatch into legless maggots (grubs). Later the maggots pupate to become adult flies.

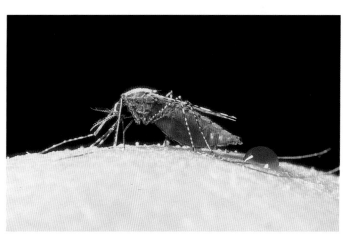

▲ CARRYING DISEASES

Mosquitoes (Culicdae) suck human and animal blood. This one is feeding from a human being. Using its needle-like mouthparts, the mosquito pierces its victim's skin to suck up blood. These insects can infect their prey with deadly diseases, including malaria and yellow fever.

121

Dragonflies

The order Odonata contains dragonflies and damselflies. It is a small order with just 5,000 species in total. Dragonflies and damselflies are found wetlands worldwide, both tropical and temperate. Odonata means 'toothed' and refers to their sharp, pointed jaws. Dragonflies are large, slender insects. Their relatives, damselflies, are smaller and more delicate. Both dragonflies and damselflies come in many bright colours, including scarlet, blue and green.

Like bugs, dragonflies undergo incomplete metamorphosis, hatching as nymphs and gradually become more like adults. Both nymphs and adults are carnivores and expert hunters, but adults and young live in very different ways. Nymphs grow up underwater in ponds and streams. Adults are one of the largest winged insects and are powerful fliers.

▲ LARGE EYES

Dragonflies have extremely large compound eyes, as this close-up shows. The eyes cover most of the insect's head and almost meet at the top. Each compound eye has up to 30,000 lenses, each of which may help to build up a detailed picture. Dragonflies can detect movement easily and use their keen sight to track down their prey.

◀ FLYING CHAMP

Dragonflies are among the fastest insect fliers. They can race along at speeds of up to 95km/h. Unlike other insects, their wings move independently. As each wing circles, it makes a figure of eight. This helps the insect to accelerate, brake and hover in one place – and also to steer with great accuracy.

Dragonfly
(Trithemis annulata)

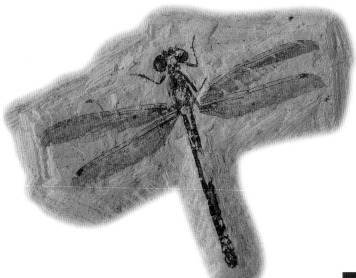

◄ ANCIENT INSECTS

Dragonflies are an ancient group of insects. From fossils, scientists have discovered that they flew on Earth 300 million years ago. They existed before the age of the dinosaurs. Some prehistoric dragonflies were giant insects, with wings that measured up to 60cm across. No known modern species comes close to that size.

NIFTY HUNTER ►

A dragonfly feeds on a fly. It uses its sharp, pointed jaws to tear its prey into tiny chunks. Dragonflies often hunt in flight. They hold their spindly legs in front to form a small catching basket. Any flying insects within reach are quickly bagged. The dragonfly will sometimes even consume its prey in mid-flight.

◄ GROWING UP

Clinging to a plant stem, a young damselfly emerges from its final moult by a pond. Both dragonflies and damselflies lay their eggs in fresh water. The young hunt, feed and grow underwater. Gills on their abdomens allow them to extract oxygen from the water like fish. When fully grown, the nymph crawls up a plant stem and then moults for the last time. As its skin splits, the young adult climbs out.

DRYING OUT ►

A young dragonfly rests after emerging from its moulted skin. Its short, crumpled wings and abdomen gradually lengthen and harden as blood is pumped into them. Its body colours will also appear soon. Adult dragonflies live only a few weeks, during which time they will mate and lay eggs.

Fleas, Grasshoppers and Mantids

Most beetles and bugs rely on the power of flight, but these three orders of insects have evolved different methods of moving around. Fleas are tiny, wingless parasites. Their strong muscles make them champion leapers. Fleas live on warm-blooded mammals and birds, and drink their blood. They belong to the order Siphonaptera, which refers to their sucking mouthparts and lack of wings.

Grasshoppers are also powerful leapers, well known for the loud, chirping noises they sing to attract a mate. These insects belong to the order Orthoptera, which means 'straight wings'. The grasshopper family includes crickets and locusts. Most grasshoppers are plant-eaters.

Mantids belong to the order Dictyoptera, and all are carnivores. These large insects are disguised to blend in with their surroundings. This superb camouflage helps them catch their prey. Unlike grasshoppers and fleas, mantids are found mainly in warm countries.

▲ HIGH JUMP CHAMPION

With no wings, fleas cannot fly. They are, however, amazing leapers. A flea can jump 30cm high – 130 times its own height. If humans could leap as high as fleas, we would be able to jump over tall buildings! The incredible leaping ability of a flea allows it to hop on to much larger animals as they pass by.

DEADLY PEST ▶

A rat flea (right) feeds on human blood. Different species of fleas are designed to feed on certain types of animals. If hungry, however, a flea will suck any animal's blood. By feeding from various hosts (victims), fleas pass on diseases. In medieval times, they carried a terrible disease called bubonic plague. Known as the Black Death, it killed half the population of Europe. The fleas carried the disease after biting infected rats.

SPINY LEGS ▶

This close-up of a mantis shows the insect's spiny front legs. It uses its forelegs to capture insects, which it then eats alive. The mantis lurks among flowers or leaves, waiting for passing insects. When a victim gets close enough, the mantis lunges forward to grab its next meal.

Praying mantis
(*Mantis religiosa*)

Grasshopper
(Acrididae)

◀ ONE GIANT LEAP

Grasshoppers escape from their enemies by leaping, as this one is doing. These insects have two pairs of wings but are not strong fliers. They can cover up to 1m in one single bound. Before it leaps, the grasshopper gathers its strong hind legs under its body. Muscles then pull on the upper and lower legs to straighten the limbs and hurl the insect into the air.

FLOWER DISGUISE ▶

Mantids use their camouflage to hunt down their prey. This beautiful tropical 'flower' is actually a flower mantis. These amazing insects have flaps on their legs and heads that resemble the petals of flowers. Some mantids mimic green or dying leaves.

◀ SINGING

This male grasshopper is stridulating (singing) to attract a female. He produces a stream of high-pitched rasping sounds by rubbing his hind legs against his front wings. Crickets sing in a slightly different way – they rub rough patches on their wings together. These insects can detect sound through special 'ears' on their legs or abdomens.

Beetles, Bugs and People

Beetles and bugs do many useful jobs that benefit people, either directly or indirectly. They fertilize plants and consume waste matter. They also provide a valuable food source for many other animals, including reptiles and birds.

However, most people regard many beetles and bugs as pests because they can harm us or our lands and possessions. Aphids, chafers and weevils attack cropfields, orchards, vegetable plots and gardens. Woodboring beetles damage timber, furniture, carpets and clothes. Blood-sucking bugs harm humans and livestock, and some carry dangerous diseases, such as malaria. People wage war against these pests — and many other harmless beetles and bugs. Some species are in danger of dying out altogether because people are killing them, or destroying the places in which they live.

▲ CARPET-CRUNCHER

A carpet beetle larva munches on a woollen carpet. These young beetles become pests when they hatch out on carpets and clothes. The larvae have spines on their bodies that protect them from enemies. A close relative, the museum beetle, also causes havoc. It eats its way through preserved animal specimens in museums.

COLLECTING INSECTS ▶

If you are collecting insects, remember to handle them carefully so that you do not damage them. Always return insects to the place where you found them. Do not try to catch delicate insects such as dragonflies, or ones that could sting you, such as wasps.

▲ DUTCH ELM DISEASE

Elm bark beetles (*Scolytus scolytus*) are wood-borers. The fungus they carry causes Dutch elm disease, which kills elm trees. During the 1970s, a major outbreak of the disease destroyed most of the elm trees in Britain.

Manna from Heaven

The Old Testament of the Bible tells how the ancient Israelites survived in the desert by eating 'manna'. After many centuries of debate, historians now believe this strange food may have been scale insects, living on tamarisk trees.

▲ WOODWORM DAMAGE

This chair has fallen prey to woodworm. These beetles (Anobiidae family) can literally reduce wood to powder. Laid as eggs inside the timber, the young feed on the wood until they are ready to pupate. As winged adults, they quickly bore their way to freedom, leaving tell-tale exit holes in the wood.

▲ GARDENERS' FRIEND

These black bean aphids (*Aphis fabae*) are infested with tiny parasitic wasps. The female wasp lays her eggs on the aphids. When the young hatch, they eat the bugs. Gardeners consider aphids a pest and welcome the wasps in their gardens. Wasps are sometimes used in large numbers by gardeners to control pests.

BUTTERFLIES AND MOTHS

What is the difference between a butterfly and a moth? It's not easy to answer this question. Butterflies tend to be brightly coloured and fly by day, while moths usually have drab colours and fly at night. A moth's antennae are feathery or thread-like, but a butterfly's antennae are shaped like clubs, with a lump at the end. But there are many exceptions and in some countries butterflies and moths are not split into separate groups at all. The special features of butterflies and moths are their long, hollow feeding tube, called a proboscis, and the dust-like scales that cover their wide, flat wings. There may be as many as 200 to 600 scales per square millimetre of wing.

Winged Beauties

Butterflies and moths are the most beautiful of all insects. On sunny days, butterflies flit from flower to flower. Their slow, fluttering flight often reveals the full glory of their large, vividly coloured wings. Moths are usually less brightly coloured than butterflies and generally fly at night. Together, butterflies and moths make up one of the largest orders (groups) of insects, called Lepidoptera. This order includes more than 165,000 different species, of which 20,000 are types of butterfly and 145,000 are types of moth. The richest variety is found in tropical forests, but there are butterflies and moths in fields, woods, grasslands, deserts and mountains in every area of land in the world – except Antarctica.

Geometrid moth
(Hypochrosis bifurcata)

Body cover[ed]
in thick ha[ir]

Feathery
antennae.

▲ MOTHS

Most moths fly only at dusk or at night. They rest on tree trunks and leaf litter by day, where their generally drab colours make them difficult to see. Moths tend to have plump bodies covered in thick hair, and their antennae are feathery or thread-like.

▼ RESTING BUTTERFLY

You can usually tell a butterfly from a moth by the way it folds its wings when it is resting. A moth spreads its wings back like a tent, with only the upper sides visible. However, a butterfly settles with its wings folded flat with the uppersides together, so that only the undersides show.

Green-veined white butterfly
(Pieris napi)

Psyche and Aphrodite
The Ancient Greeks believed that, after death, their souls fluttered away from their bodies in the form of butterflies. The Greek symbol for the soul was a butterfly-winged girl called Psyche. According to legend, Aphrodite (goddess of love) was jealous of Psyche's beauty. She ordered her son Eros to make Psyche fall in love with him. Instead, Eros fell in love with her himself.

Blue Morpho butterfly
(*Morpho peleides*)

Antenna.

Compound eye
consists of up to
about 6,000
individual lenses.

Brightly coloured
forewing.

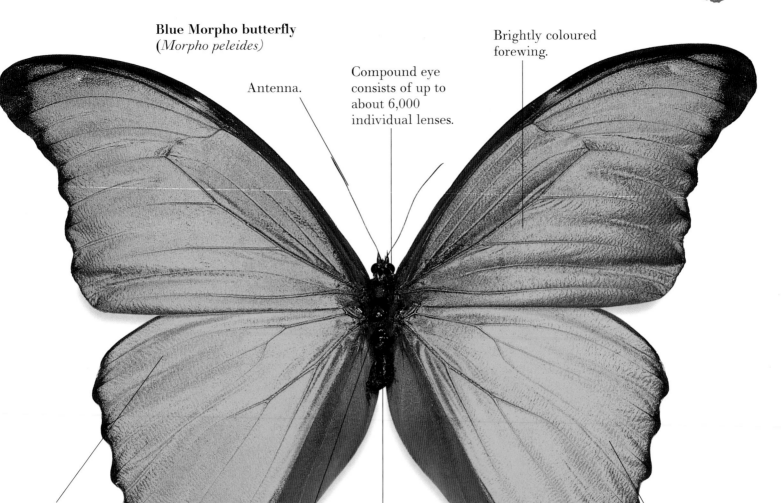

Wing is
covered in
overlapping
scales.

Tough outer coating
supports the body,
instead of an
internal skeleton.

Typical slim
body of a
butterfly.

The hindwing
is smaller than
the forewing.

▲ FEATURES OF A BUTTERFLY

Butterflies tend to have brilliantly coloured wings
and fly only during the day. They have slim bodies
without much hair, and their antennae are shaped
like clubs, with a lump at the end. However, the
distinction between butterflies and moths is quite
blurred, and in some countries they are not
distinguished at all.

▶ CATERPILLARS

A many-legged caterpillar hatches from
a butterfly's egg. When young, both
moths and butterflies are
caterpillars. Only
when they are big
enough do the
caterpillars go
through the
changes that
turn them into
winged adults.

Privet Hawk moth caterpillar
(*Sphinx ligustri*)

Did you know? Tiger moths make high-pitched clicks at night to warn bats they taste bad.

How Butterflies Look

Butterflies vary enormously in size and shape. In regions such as Europe and the United States they range from big butterflies such as the Monarch, which has a wingspan of 10cm, to the Small Blue, which is tinier than a postage stamp. The variation among tropical species is even greater. The largest butterfly in the world is the rare Queen Alexandra's Birdwing. The female has a wingspan of 28cm, which is more than 25 times the size of the minute Western Pygmy Blue. The shape of butterfly wings can be deceptive. In photographs and drawings, butterflies are usually shown with both pairs of wings stretched out fully. However, they are not always seen like this in nature. For example, sometimes the forewings may hide the hindwings.

A male Queen Alexandra's Birdwing butterfly has brightly coloured wings.

Monarch butterfly
(Danaus plexippus)

◄ **MONARCH MIGRATIONS**
The Monarch is one of the biggest butterflies outside of tropical regions. In North America it makes long journeys, called migrations, to spend the winter in warm areas such as California, Florida and Mexico. Some Monarch butterflies fly from as far away as Canada.

▼ **COMMA BUTTERFLY**
Each species of butterfly has its own distinctive wing markings. The Comma butterfly gets its name from the small, white C or comma-shape on the undersides of its hindwings.

Comma butterfly
(Polygonia c-album)

▼ BIG AS A BIRD

The Queen Alexandra's Birdwing is a rare butterfly that lives only in the Northern Province of Papua New Guinea. Its wings are wider than those of many birds. Females can grow up to 28cm across.

Queen Alexandra's Birdwing butterfly
(*Ornithoptera alexandrae*)

The bright yellow body warns predators that the butterfly is poisonous.

Small Blue butterfly
(*Cupido minimus*)

▲ SMALL BLUE

The Small Blue is the smallest butterfly in Great Britain. It is barely 2cm across, even when fully grown. However, the tiny Pygmy Blue butterfly of North America is even smaller with a wingspan of between 11 and 18mm.

Peacock butterfly
(*Inachis io*)

► PEACOCK EYES

The Peacock butterfly is easily identified by the pairs of markings on both the front and hindwings. These large spots look like eyes. It is one of the most common and distinctive butterflies in Europe and parts of Asia, including Japan.

Swallowtail butterfly
(*Papilio machaon*)

► A TAIL OF DECEPTION

The wing shapes of butterflies can vary dramatically from species to species. Many butterflies in the family called Papilionidae have distinctive tails on their wings, a bit like swallows' tails. Some species of Swallowtail use them to confuse predators. When the wings are folded, the tails look like antennae, so a predator may mistake the butterfly's tail-end for its head.

133

How Moths Look

American Moon moth
(Actias luna)

Like butterflies, moths come in all shapes and sizes. There is also more variety in wing shape amongst moths than amongst butterflies. In terms of size, some of the smallest species of moth have wingspans no wider than 3mm. The biggest have wings that are almost as wide as this book, for example the Hercules moth of Australia and New Guinea and the Bent-wing Ghost moth of South-east Asia. The larvae (caterpillars) of small moths may be tiny enough to live inside seeds, fruits, stems, leaves and flowers. The caterpillars of larger moths are bigger, although some do live inside tree trunks and other stems.

▲ **MOON MOTH**
The American Moon moth shows just how delicate and attractive large moths can be. Its wingspan is about 32cm and it has long, slender tails on its hindwings. When it is resting on a tree, its body and head are so well hidden by its big wings that any predatory bird will peck harmlessly at its tails. This allows the moth time to escape.

▼ **ELEPHANT HAWK MOTH**
Many moths are less colourful than butterflies, but they are not all drably coloured. For example, the Elephant Hawk moth is a beautiful insect with delicate pink wings that blend in well with its favourite flowers (valerian and pink honeysuckle). However, the Elephant Hawk moth flies at night so it is not often seen in its full glory.

Garden Tiger moth
(Arctia caja)

◄ **COLOUR RANGE**
Identifying moths can be quite difficult, as some species show a wide range of colouring. For example, many Garden Tiger moths are slightly different colours from each other. As a result of this variety, scientists often use the Garden Tiger moth for breeding experiments.

Elephant Hawk moth *(Deilephila elpenor)*

134

▶ INDIAN MOTH

This moth belongs to the family Pyralidae and comes from southern India. This tiny moth has a wingspan of just 2cm. The distinctive white bands on its wings break up the moth's outline and make it more difficult to spot when at rest.

Lepyrodes neptis

Did you know? The Big Beet Borer (Melitta gloriosa) has a furry striped abdomen and looks like a bee.

▼ WIDE WINGS

The Giant Atlas moth of India and South-east Asia is one of the world's largest moths. Only the Giant Agrippa moth of South America has wider wings, with a span of up to 30cm. Some Atlas moths can grow to almost 45cm when their wings are opened fully. They have shiny triangles on their wings that are thought to confuse predators by reflecting light.

Giant Atlas moth
(Archaeoattacus edwardsi)

▲ MANY PLUME MOTH

The beautiful feathery wings of this unusual looking moth give it its name, the Many Plume moth (*Alucita hexadactyla*). Each of its fore and hindwings is split into six slender feathery sections, or plumes.

▼ LARGE CATERPILLAR

Caterpillars have many different shapes and sizes, just like moths. The young Acacia Emperor moth is one of the biggest caterpillars. Although they are generally sausage-shaped, some caterpillars are twig-like, making them hard to see in a bush or tree.

135

Body Parts

In many ways, butterflies and moths are similar to other insects. Their bodies are divided into three parts – the head, the thorax and the abdomen. The mouth, eyes and antennae (feelers) are situated on the head. The thorax is the body's powerhouse, driving the legs and wings. The abdomen is where food is digested. Like all insects, butterflies and moths have bodies, which are covered by a tough outer shell, called an exoskeleton. However, butterflies and moths also have unique features, such as their big, flat wings and a long proboscis (tongue).

Abdomen

▲ EGG CENTRE

The abdomen (rear section) houses a butterfly's digestive system. It also produces eggs in female butterflies and moths, and sperm in males.

◄ SWEET SUCKING

This butterfly is feeding on a prickly pear cactus fruit in Mexico. Butterflies and moths feed mainly on nectar and other sweet juices. They suck them up through a long tube-like tongue called a proboscis. Butterflies and moths have no jaws.

► CONNECTED WINGS

The forewings and hindwings of most moths overlap. Although each pair of wings is separate, they act together because long bristles on the hindwing catch on to hooks on the underside of the forewing, rather like a doorlatch.

Burnet moth with wings raised, showing the bristle linking the forewing and hindwing.

▲ FEEDING STRAW

A Purple Emperor butterfly rolls out its proboscis to feed. The proboscis stretches out almost as long as its body. When a butterfly rests, it rolls up its long proboscis beneath its head. Hawk moths have the longest proboscises.

► MOTH WINGS

Butterflies and moths each have
two pairs of large, flat wings
and three pairs of legs. The
wings and legs are attached
to the thorax (the
mid-section of the body).
The two pairs of wings
are not always visible.

One of the pair of
large flat forewings.

Moths and
butterflies need
powerful
thoraxes to flap
their huge wings.

Emperor moth
(Saturnia pavonia)

The hindwings
are normally
covered by
the forewings
when at rest.

Wings click up.

Thorax clicks down.

Wings click down.

Thorax clicks up.

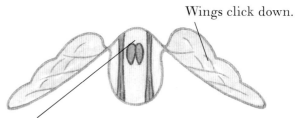

▲ SENSITIVE FEET

Moths and butterflies taste with their tarsi (feet).
When they land on a flower, they will not unroll the
tongue to feed unless their foot sense the sweetness
of nectar. Females stamp their tarsi on leaves to
decide if they are ripe for egg-laying. They will lay
eggs only if the leaves release the correct scent.

▲ FLIGHT

The wings are joined to the thorax (mid-
section). Muscles pull the top of the
thorax down, making the wings flip up
Then the muscles pull the thorax in,
making it thinner so the top clicks back
up again, flipping the wings down.

137

European Map butterfly
(*Araschnia levana*)

Scaly Wings

The scientific name for butterflies and moths, Lepidoptera, refers to the minute scales covering their wings. *Lepis* is the Ancient Greek word for scale and *pteron* means wing. The scales are actually flattened hairs and each one is connected to the wings by a short stalk. These delicate scales give butterfly wings their amazing colours, but can rub off easily like dust. Underneath the scales, butterfly and moth wings are transparent like the wings of other insects. The vivid colours of the scales come either from pigments (coloured chemicals) in the scales or the way their structure reflects light.

▲ SCENTED SCALES

Many male butterflies have special scales called *androconia* that help them to attract mates. These scales scent the wing with an odour that stimulates females.

▲ OVERLAPPING SCALES

Tiny scales overlap and completely coat the wing. They are so loosely attached that they often shake off in flight.

▲ CELL SPACE

The areas between the wing veins are called cells. All the cells radiate outwards from one vein at the base of the wing.

Black-veined
White butterfly
(*Aporia crataegi*)

▼ WING VEINS

Butterfly and moth wings are supported by a framework of veins. These veins are filled with air, nerve fibres and blood. The pattern of the veins helps to classify butterflies and moths into a number of families.

Highly visible veins of a Black-veined White butterfly.

► SCALING DOWN

A Large White butterfly takes off from a buttercup. Butterflies in flight naturally lose scales from time to time. The loss does not seem to harm some species. However, others find themselves unable to fly without a reasonable coating of scales to soak up the sun and warm up their bodies.

Did you know? The wings of the Glasswing butterfly are transparent, making it almost invisible.

◄ MORPHO WING

The metallic blue wings of the South American Morpho butterfly shimmer in the sunlight. This effect is produced by the special way the surface texture of their wings reflects light. When filmed by a video camera that is sensitive to invisible ultraviolet light, these scales flash like a beacon.

► EYE TO EYE

The patterns of scales on some butterflies form circles that resemble the bold, staring eyes of a larger animal. Scientists think that these eyespots may have developed to startle and scare away predators such as birds. However, the eyespots on other butterflies may be used to attract mates.

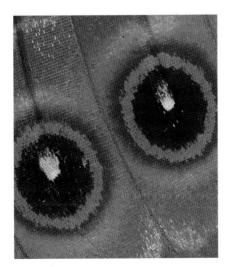

Butterfly Ball
The butterfly's fragile beauty has always inspired artists. In the 1800s, many European artists portrayed them as fairies, with human bodies and butterfly's wings.

Focus on

SUN LOVERS

Butterflies and moths can only fly if their body temperature reaches at least 25–30°C. If they are too cold, the muscles powering the wings do not work. To warm up, butterflies bask in the sun, so that the wing scales soak up sunlight like solar panels. Night-flying moths shiver their wings to warm them instead.

Butterflies and moths fly in a different way from other insects. They fly in a similar way to birds. Most insects simply beat their wings very rapidly to move through the air. Since they can only stay aloft if they beat their wings fast enough, they soon run out of energy. However, many butterflies ripple their wings slowly up and down. Some, such as the white admiral, can even glide on currents of air with just an occasional flap to keep them aloft. This enables them to fly amazing distances. Flight patterns vary from the fluttering of the wood white to the soaring of the purple emperor butterflies. Wingbeat tends to be faster in the smaller species, with the skipper family having the fastest wingbeat of all. Moths, such as the hawk moths with their jet plane-like wings, fly at fast speeds in a generally straight line.

TWISTERS

To the human eye, the wings of butterflies and moths appear simply to flap. However, freeze-frame photography reveals that the bases of the wings twist as they move up and down, so that the wing tips move in a figure of eight.

Butterflies look like clumsy fliers, but their acrobatic twists and turns enable them to escape sparrows and other predatory birds. Some moths can fly at up to 48 km/h when frightened.

Flight

the wings push air backwards

the butterfly is propelled forwards

a butterfly lifts its wings upwards

as the wings come down again, they provide lift to keep the butterfly up

UP, UP AND AWAY

The wings are stiff along the front edges and at the bases, but the rest of the wing is bendy. The stiff front edges of the wing give the butterfly lift, like the wings of an aircraft, as it flies forward. The flexing of the rest of the wing pushes air backwards and drives the butterfly forwards.

GRACEFUL GLIDERS

Butterflies in the family *Nymphalidae*, such as this painted lady (*Vanessa cardui*), flap their wings occasionally when in flight. They glide along, with just the odd beat of their wings.

Senses

Butterflies and moths have a very different range of senses from humans. Instead of having just two eyes they have compound eyes, made up of hundreds or even thousands of tiny lenses. They also have incredibly sensitive antennae (feelers) which they use not only to smell food, but also to hear and feel things. The antennae play a vital part in finding a mate and deciding where to lay eggs. They may even detect taste and temperature change. Butterflies and moths have a good sense of taste and smell in their tarsi (feet), too. Moths hear sounds with a form of ears called tympanal organs. These little membranes are situated on the thorax or abdomen and vibrate like a drum when sound hits them.

▲ ANTENNAE
The feathery side branches on an Atlas moth's antennae increase the surface area for detecting scent, like the spikes on a TV aerial. They allow the male moth to pinpoint certain smells, such as the scent of a potential mate, at huge distances.

▲ SMELL THE WIND
A butterfly's antennae act like an external nose packed with highly sensitive smell receptors. They can pick up minute traces of chemicals in the air that are undetectable to the human nose.

◀ ATTRACTIVE ANTENNAE
Male Longhorn moths (*Adelidae*) have very long antennae. These antennae are used to pick up scent, but they also have another, very different, job. They shine in the sunlight and attract females when the males dance up and down in the afternoon.

Moth's head

A noctuid moth showing the position of the ears at the rear of the thorax.

▲ HEARING BODY

Many moths have "ears" made up of tiny membranes stretched over little cavities. These ears are situated on the thorax. When the membranes are vibrated by a sound, a nerve sends a signal to the brain. These ears are highly sensitive to the high-pitched sounds of bats, which prey on moths.

Did you know? The male Emperor moth can smell a female at 11km – upwind!

◄ MULTI-VISION

The compound eyes of an Orange-tip butterfly are large. The thousands of lenses in a compound eye each form their own picture of the world. The butterfly's brain puts the images together into one picture. Although butterflies are quite short-sighted, they can see all round using their multiple eyes.

▼ FEELING FOR FLOWERS

Butterflies and moths find the flowers they want to feed on mainly by the incredibly sensitive sense of smell their antennae give them. This enables them to pick up the scent of a single bloom from some distance away.

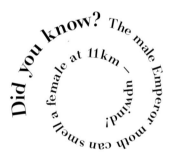

▼ A CASE OF THE BLUES

Butterflies don't see flowers such as this evening primrose the way we do, for their eyes are not very sensitive to red and yellow light. But they can see ultraviolet light, which we cannot see. They see flowers in the colours shown here.

143

Eggs

Butterflies and moths begin life as tiny eggs. After mating, some females simply scatter their eggs as they fly. However, most females seek a suitable place to fix their eggs, either individually or in batches of up to 1,000 or more. The leaves or stem of particular plants are common sites since they will provide food for the caterpillars after hatching. A female butterfly uses her sensitive antennae to locate the correct plant species. She stamps or scratches the leaves with her feet to check that the scent is right and that no other butterfly has laid eggs there before. Once she has laid her eggs, the female flies off almost straight away.

Eggs emerge through the ovipositor.

Large White butterfly
(Pieris brassicae)

▲ **EGG OOZE**

A female butterfly pushes her eggs out, one by one, through her ovipositor (the egg-laying duct at the end of her abdomen). The eggs ooze out in a kind of glue that sticks them in place as it hardens.

A Peacock butterfly's eggs, laid on the underside of a nettle leaf.

▲ **RIDGED EGG**

The egg of the Painted Lady butterfly has a glassy shell with elaborate ridges. The shape of the egg is fairly constant in each family.

▲ **EGG SITE**

A Peacock butterfly has laid her eggs on a sheltered part of the plant. This will provide them with warmth and protection, as well as food. Many butterflies and moths lay their eggs in random patterns, which improves the chances of predatory insects missing some of them.

144

▼ EGGS IN CLOSE-UP

The moth eggs shown here are red-brown and poisonous. However, most eggs are dull green or yellow in colour. This helps them to blend into their background so that they remain hidden from predators. Different types of egg are smooth, shiny or patterned.

◄ EGG SHAPES

The eggs of a Large White butterfly are lozenge-shaped. Butterfly eggs vary in shape from the spiny balls of the White Admiral to the cones of the Silver-spotted Skipper. All have a hard shell lined on the inside with wax, which protects the developing caterpillar inside.

▲ DIFFERENT NESTS

Some moths lay their eggs along a grass stem, so they look like the stem itself. Others lay eggs in dangling strings or in overlapping rows like tiles on a roof.

► HATCHING EGGS

Most butterfly eggs hatch within a few days of being laid. However, a few types of egg pass an entire winter before hatching. They hatch when temperatures begin to rise and the caterpillars stand a chance of survival. The eggs grow darker in colour just before hatching. The tiny caterpillars bite their way out from their shells. Their minute jaws cut a circle in the shell that is just big enough for the head to squeeze through.

Newly hatched caterpillars of the Large White butterfly.

145

The Caterpillar

Five-spotted Hawk moth caterpillar

Once a caterpillar (or larva) bites its way from the egg, it immediately begins eating. While most adult butterflies and moths survive on nectar, a caterpillar chomps it ways through leaves, fruits and stems. It grows rapidly, shedding its skin several times as it swells. Within a month, it may be fully grown and ready to change into a butterfly or moth. Caterpillars are far more numerous than adult butterflies and moths because most are eaten by predators or killed by diseases. They hide among vegetation and crevices in bark, often feeding at night to avoid danger.

Head

True legs

Thorax

Abdomen

Spine or horn at the tip of the abdomen.

Each proleg ends in a ring of crochets (hooks) that hold on to stems and leaves.

Anal proleg or clasper enables a caterpillar to cling on to plants.

◀ CATERPILLAR PARTS

Caterpillars have big heads with strong jaws for snipping off food. Their long, soft bodies are divided into thirteen segments. The front segments become the thorax in the adult insect and the rear segments become the abdomen.

PROLEGS ▶

The caterpillar of an Emperor Gum moth (*Antheraea eucalypti*) has five pairs of prolegs (false legs) on its abdomen. All caterpillars have these prolegs, which they lose as an adult. Caterpillars also have three pairs of true legs, which become the legs of the adult.

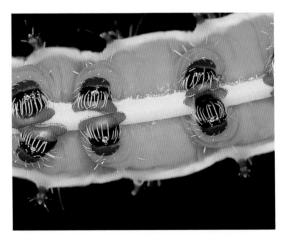

146

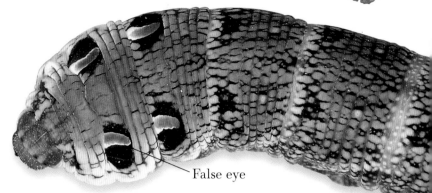

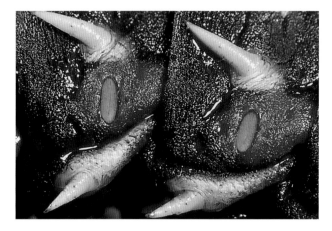

False eye

▲ **BREATHING HOLES**

A caterpillar does not have lungs for breathing like humans. Instead, it has tiny holes called spiracles that draw oxygen into the body tissues. There are several spiracles on either side of the caterpillar.

▲ **FALSE EYES**

The large eye shapes behind the head of an Elephant Hawk moth caterpillar are actually false eyes for scaring predators. In fact, caterpillars can barely see at all. They possess six small eyes that can only distinguish between dark and light.

Did you know? Caterpillars can close up their spiracles and survive underwater for hours.

◄ **CHANGING SKIN**

Every week or so, the skin of a growing caterpillar grows too tight. It then splits down the back to reveal a new skin underneath. At first the new skin is soft and stretchy. As the caterpillar sheds its old skin, it swells the new one by taking in air through its spiracles (air holes). It then lies still for a few hours while the new large skin hardens.

◄ **FLY ATTACK**

A Puss Moth caterpillar can defend itself against predators. It puffs up its front and whips its tail like a tiny dragon, before spraying a jet of poison over its foe.

SILK MAKERS ►

Peacock butterfly caterpillars live and feed in web-like tents. They spin these tents from silken thread. All caterpillars can produce this sticky liquid from the spinneret under their mouth. The silk helps them to hold on to surfaces as they move about.

Tunnel left by leaf-mining caterpillar.

Hungry Caterpillars

Caterpillars are incredible eating machines, munching their way through several times their own body weight of food in a single day. This is why they grow so rapidly. Their first meal is usually the egg from which they hatch. Once that is gone, they move on to the nearest food source. Some eat nearby unhatched eggs and a few even eat other caterpillars. Most feed on the leaves and stems of their own particular food plant. This is usually the plant on which they hatched. However, some moth caterpillars eat wool or cotton. The food is stored in the caterpillar's body and is used for growth and energy in the later stages of its development. The caterpillar stage lasts for at least two weeks, and sometimes very much longer.

▲ LEAF MINING

Many tiny caterpillars eat their way through the inside of the leaf instead of crawling across the surface. This activity is known as leaf mining. Often, their progress is revealed by a pale tunnel beneath the leaf surface.

Swallowtail butterfly caterpillar
(*Papilio machaon*)

Sensitive palps are located near the mouth.

The true legs are used to grip foliage

▲ FEEDING HABITS

Caterpillars eat different food plants from those used by the adults. Swallowtail butterfly caterpillars feed on fennel, carrots and milk-parsley. Adult swallowtail butterflies drink the nectar of thistles and buddleias.

▶ IDENTIFYING FOOD

The head end of a Privet Hawk moth caterpillar is shown in close-up here. A caterpillar probably identifies food using sensitive organs called palps that are just in front of the mouth.

◀ FAST EATERS

Cabbages are the main food plants of the Large White caterpillar. These insects can strip a field of foliage in a few nights. This is why many farmers and gardeners kill caterpillars with pesticides. However, their numbers may be controlled naturally by parasitic wasps so long as the wasps are not killed by pesticides.

Alice in Wonderland

In Lewis Carroll's magical story Alice in Wonderland, *a pipe-smoking caterpillar discusses with Alice what it is like to change size. Carroll was probably thinking of how caterpillars grow in stages.*

▲ PICKY EATER

Many caterpillars feed on trees. Some, such as the Gypsy moth caterpillars, feed on almost any tree, but others are more fussy. This Cecropia moth caterpillar feeds only on willow trees.

▲ PROCESSIONARY CATERPILLARS

The caterpillars of Processionary moths travel to feeding areas in a neat row. They also rest together in silken nests. These insects are poisonous and so do not try to hide as others do.

Focus on

Moth caterpillars ooze out a silky liquid thread from ducts called spinnerets. One species produces a liquid so strong and fine that it can be used in silk, one of the most beautiful and luxurious of all fabrics. This caterpillar, that of the *Bombyx mori* moth, is known as the silk worm. In China, it has been cultivated for its silk for almost 5,000 years. According to legend, in about 2,700BC the Chinese princess Si-Ling-Chi first discovered how to use the silk worm's cocoon to make silk thread. She was known thereafter as *Seine-Than* (the Silk Goddess).

1 The caterpillar of the silk moth, (*Bombyx mori*) feeds entirely on the leaves of just one plant, the mulberry tree. Today, silk worms do not live in the wild. They are farmed and fed on pre-chopped mulberry leaves.

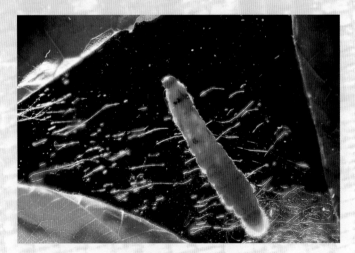

2 When the caterpillar is ready to change into an adult moth, it finds a suitable spot between the mulberry leaves. Once settled, it begins to ooze silk thread from its spinneret.

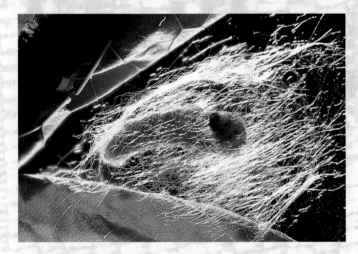

3 At first, the silk forms just a flimsy curtain, with only a few threads strung between the leaves. The caterpillar is still clearly visible at this stage.

Making Silk

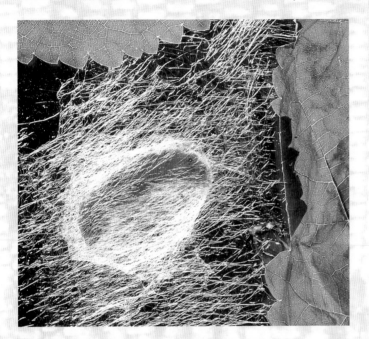

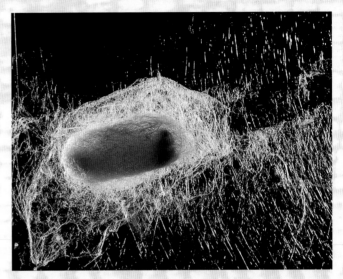

5 Inside the cocoon, the caterpillar becomes a pupa (also known as a chrysalis). This is a stage in the development of moths and butterflies when they neither feed nor move. They emerge from this stage as adult insects.

4 After a few hours the caterpillar stops running the silk between the leaves and begins to wrap itself round and round. It uses almost a kilometre of silk to completely encase itself in a cocoon of the gummy thread.

6 Only a few pupae are allowed to emerge as adult *Bombyx mori* moths for breeding. Most cocoons are plunged into boiling water, which kills the pupa and dissolves the gum on the silk. The fine silk from several cocoons is twisted together to make usable silk thread.

Pupae

Caterpillar of Large Tortoiseshell butterfly shedding its skin as it becomes a pupa.

After about a month of eating and growing, a caterpillar is ready to pupate (become a pupa). This is when it transforms into an adult butterfly or moth. Pupae are defenceless, so many moth caterpillars spin a silken cocoon around themselves for protection. Many others tunnel into the ground before pupating. Most butterfly pupae are naked, but they are generally well camouflaged or hidden in leaf litter. Cocoons look lifeless, but inside there is continuous activity as the caterpillar gradually transforms itself. This process, called metamorphosis, can take just a few days, although in some species it may be over a year before the adult insect finally emerges.

◀ **HANGING ON**

Many butterfly caterpillars stick themselves on to branches and stems with a pad of silk before pupating. Then they shed their old skin without dropping to the ground. Other caterpillars bury themselves in the soil or leaf litter.

▲ **HIBERNATING PUPA**

Some pupae, such as this Brown Hairstreak butterfly, complete their development in a couple of weeks. Other species pass the winter in a state of suspended development called diapause. This is very common among temperate butterflies and moths.

Pupa sticking upwards, held in place by a silk thread.

▶ **UP OR DOWN**

The pupae of White and Swallowtail butterflies stick upwards, held in place by a silk thread around the middle. These are called succinct pupae. Other pupae hang head-down from branches. They are called suspended pupae.

Elephant Hawk moth pupa with wing veins visible through the surface.

Old skin shed during the caterpillar's transformation into a pupa.

◀ DEVELOPING PUPA

The outlines of the wings, legs and antennae are faintly visible on the surface of the pupa showing that it is almost ready to hatch. Inside, the tissues that made up the caterpillar's body dissolve, ready for rebuilding as an adult.

FAILED PROTECTION ▶

The pupa of this Emperor moth (*Saturnia pavonia*) has been eaten away from the inside by the larva of a parasitic fly. The cocoon has been cut away to reveal the hole from which the fly grub has emerged. Pupae are never completely safe from predators.

Hole in moth pupa.

Pupa of parasite.

The Butterfly Lovers

An old Chinese tale tells of Zhu Yingtai, who disguises herself as a boy to go to college. There, she falls in love with Liang Shanbo. But Liang is unaware she is a girl and Zhu is forced to marry a rich man's son. Liang realises his mistake and dies broken-hearted. When Zhu hears, she takes her life in despair. The gods take pity and the pair are reunited as butterflies.

Did you know? Some pupae resemble dead leaves or even bird droppings to trick predators.

Moth just hatched from pupa in cocoon.

▶ EMERGING ADULT

Butterfly pupae vary considerably in colour and shape. Some Fritillary butterfly pupae have shiny patches that look like raindrops, but most moth pupae are brown or black bullet-shaped objects. Even experts find it difficult to tell the species to which they belong. Only when all the changes are complete and the moth emerges as an imago (adult) does the identity of the insect become clear.

153

Rear claspers
grip a
silken pad.

Focus on

Pupation (changing from a caterpillar to a butterfly or moth) is one of the most astonishing transformations undergone by any living creature. Inside the chrysalis, or pupa, the body parts of the caterpillar gradually dissolve. New features grow in their place, including a totally different head and body, and two pairs of wings. This whole process can take less than a week. When these changes are complete, a fully-formed imago (adult moth or butterfly) emerges almost magically from the nondescript pouch.

1 The Monarch butterfly caterpillar (*Danaus plexippus*) spins a silken pad on a plant stem and grips it firmly with its rear claspers. It then sheds its skin to reveal the chrysalis, which clings to the silken pad with tiny hooks.

2 The chrysalis of the Monarch is plump, pale and studded with golden spots. It appears lifeless except for the occasional twitch. However, changes can sometimes be vaguely seen through the skin.

Fully formed chrysalis.

Chrysalis darkens before opening.

3 The chrysalis grows dark just before the adult emerges. The wing pattern becomes visible through the skin. The butterfly then pumps body fluids to its head and thorax. Next, the chrysalis cracks open behind the head and along the front of the wing.

Metamorphosis

4 The butterfly swallows air to make itself swell up, which splits the chrysalis even more. The insect emerges shakily and hangs down, clinging tightly to the chrysalis skin.

Wings are soft and crumpled.

5 The newly emerged adult slowly pumps blood into the veins in its wings, which begin to straighten out. The insect hangs down with its head up so that the force of gravity helps to stretch the wings. After about half an hour, it reaches its full size.

Split skin of chrysalis

Wing veins with blood pumping into them.

6 The butterfly basks in the sun for an hour or two while its wings dry out and harden. After a few trial flaps of its wings, it is ready to fly away and begin its life as an adult butterfly.

The adult butterfly tests its wings before its maiden flight.

Finding a Mate

Common Blue butterfly
(Polyommatus icarus)

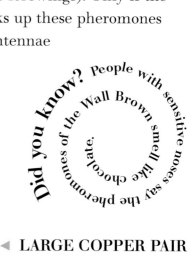

A butterfly's life is usually very short, so it has only a little while to find a mate. Most females live for just a few days, so they must begin to lay eggs as soon as possible. Male butterflies emerge from their pupae a little earlier than the females. This allows some males to mate with a newly emerged female while her wings are still soft and crumpled. However, most males court their female with elaborate flights and dances. Males and females are drawn to each other by the shape of each other's wings and by the colourful and striking patterns on them. The males also spread powerful scents that stimulate females to approach them and land alongside. Then they circle each other, performing complicated courtship dances.

▲ **COURTING BLUES**

When courting a female, a male butterfly often flutters its wings flamboyantly. It looks as if it is showing off, but it is really wafting its pheromones (the scents from special scales on its forewings). Only if the female picks up these pheromones with her antennae will she be willing to mate.

Did you know? People with sensitive noses say the pheromones of the Wall Brown smell like chocolate.

◄ **LARGE COPPER PAIR**

This pair of butterflies is about to mate. When she is ready, the female will fly away and land with her wings half open. The male will flutter down on top of her and begin to caress her abdomen with his rear end. The male then turns around to face the opposite way as they couple. The pair may remain joined like this for hours.

Madame Butterfly

One of the most famous operas is Puccini's Madame Butterfly, *written in 1904. The opera is set in the 1800s in Osaka, Japan. It tells the story of an American officer, James Pinkerton, who falls in love with a beautiful young Japanese girl. His nickname for her is Butterfly. They have a child, but Pinkerton abandons Butterfly for his wife in America. The opera ends as Butterfly dies broken-hearted.*

▼ SCENT POWER

A butterfly's scent plays a major role in attracting a mate. The scents come from glands on the abdomen of a female. On a male, the scents come from special wing scales called androconia. A male often rubs his wings over the female's antennae.

Androconia scales release scent.

▼ MALE AND FEMALE

Often, female butterflies are drab, while males are brightly coloured. The male Orange-tip, for example, has a distinctive bright orange coloured tip to its wings. However, the ends of the female Orange-tip's wings (see top right of page) are grey-black.

Male Orange-tip butterfly *(Anthocharis cardamines)*

▼ SINGLE MATE

Male butterflies mate several times in their lifetime. However a female butterfly usually mates just once and then concentrates on egg-laying. Once they have mated, many females release a special pheromone that deters other males.

Female Orange-tip butterfly *(Anthocharis cardamines)*

▲ FLYING TOGETHER

Butterflies usually stay on the ground or on a plant while coupling. But if danger threatens, they can fly off linked together, with one (called the carrier) pulling the other backwards.

157

Flower Power

Butterflies and moths have a close relationship with plants, especially with those that flower. Many live much of their lives on a particular kind of vegetation. They begin life as eggs on the plant, feed on it while they are caterpillars and change into a pupa while attached to it. Finally the adult may sip the nectar from its blooms. Just as butterflies rely on flowers for food, many flowers rely on visiting butterflies to spread their pollen. The bright colours and attractive scents of flowers may have evolved to attract butterflies and other insects such as bees. When a butterfly lands on a flower to drink nectar, grains of pollen cling to its body. Some of the pollen grains rub off on the next bloom the butterfly visits.

▲ **FEEDING ON FUCHSIA**
The caterpillar of the Elephant Hawk moth feeds on the leaves of fuchsia. Many lepidopterists (butterfly and moth experts) grow fuchsias in their gardens for the pleasure of seeing this spectacular caterpillar. However, some gardeners think of the moths as pests for the same reason.

▼ **THISTLE LOVER**
A Brimstone butterfly *(Gonepteryx rhamni)* settles on a thistle to feed. It is common throughout Europe in light woodland and in open countryside at heights of up to 2000m. The Brimstone also likes to feed on a wide range of garden flowers.

▲ **FABULOUS FUCHSIAS**
The Small Elephant Hawk moth is shown here drinking nectar from a fuchsia. Rather than settling on a flower, these large, powerful moths often feed while hovering in front of them.

▶ FEEDING TOGETHER

A group of Small Tortoiseshell butterflies *(Aglais urticae)* are shown here sipping nectar together. Small Tortoiseshells are widespread throughout Europe. They are attracted to a wide range of blooms including buddleia, Michaelmas daisy and sedum that are found in fields, by roadsides and in back gardens.

◀ STINGING NETTLES

The adult Peacock butterfly *(Inachis io)* sits on a weed called the stinging nettle. It generally feeds on flowers such as buddleia. However, the caterpillars of this species feed almost exclusively on nettles. Many gardeners clear away this unattractive weed, which causes Peacock butterflies to lay their eggs elsewhere.

Did you know? Buddleia is so attractive to many butterflies that it is sometimes called the butterfly bush.

▼ GOURMET FOOD

This beautiful Red Spotted Purple Swallowtail feeds on a desert flower in Arizona, North America. Butterflies and moths are adapted to the specific environment in which they live. Swallowtails are common throughout Europe but there they sip nectar from meadow and orchard flowers.

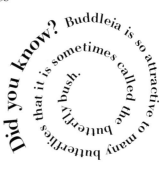

Red Spotted Purple Swallowtail butterfly *(Basilarchia astyanax)*

159

Nectar and Food

Postman butterfly
(*Heliconius*)

Butterflies and moths cannot chew food.
Instead, they suck up liquids through their long
proboscises (tongues), which act like drinking
straws. Their preferred food is nectar. This sugary
fluid is produced in the nectaries of flowers in
order to attract insects such as butterflies and bees.
Most species of butterfly survive on nectar alone
and spend most of their brief lives flitting from
flower to flower in search of this juice. Some
woodland species extract sweet liquids from a wide
variety of sources, including rotting fruit and sap
oozing from wounds in trees. A few species even
suck on dung. However, these sources do not
provide much real sustenance, which is why
butterflies rarely live for more than a few days.

▲ LONG LIFE

Heliconius butterflies of the
tropical forests of South
America are among the
few relatively long-lived
butterflies. They are able to
live for 130 days or more,
compared with barely 20
for most temperate species.
Heliconius butterflies feed
on passionfruit flowers.

▲ FRUIT EATERS

The first generation of
Comma butterflies appears
each year in early summer.
These insects feed on the
delicate white blossoms of
brambles (blackberries),
because the fruit has not
ripened at this time. The
second generation appear
in autumn, so they feed on
the ripe blackberry fruits.

Red Admiral butterfly
(*Vanessa atalanta*)

▼ CIDER DRINKING

In autumn, butterflies
such as the Red Admiral
and the Camberwell
Beauty often feed on
rotting fruit.
Sometimes the
juice has fermented
to alcohol, and the
Red Admiral may
be seen reeling
around as if
drunk.

◄ DRINKING STRAW

Many flowers hide their nectaries deep inside the blooms in order to draw the butterfly right on to their pollen sacs. Many butterflies have developed very long proboscises to reach the nectar. They probe deep into the flower to suck up the juice.

Did you know? The Purple Emperor butterfly often survives by sucking juices from the rotting bodies of dead animals.

▲ HOVERING HAWK MOTHS

The day-flying Hummingbird Hawk moth gets its name from its habit of hovering in front of flowers like a hummingbird as it sips nectar, rather than landing on the flower. The hawk moth family have the longest proboscises of all. One member, known as Darwin's Hawk moth, has a proboscis that reaches to between 30 and 35cm – about three times the length of its body.

► WOODLAND VARIETY

Many woodland butterflies extract juices from a variety of sources. The Speckled Wood butterfly sometimes sips nectar from bluebells. However, it feeds mainly on honeydew. This is the sugary secretion of tiny insects called aphids. The leaves of flowers are often coated with honeydew.

▲ NIGHT FEEDER

Noctuid moths often sip nectar from ragworts in meadows by moonlight. In temperate countries, these moths mostly feed on warm summer nights. They get their name from the Latin word *noctuis*, which means night.

Speckled Wood butterfly
(Pararge aegeria)

161

At Ground Level

Butterflies need warmth in order to fly. In tropical regions it is usually warm enough for butterflies to fly for most of the day. But in cooler countries, they often spend much of the day resting. They spread out their wings and turn with the sun to soak up the rays. Male butterflies and moths also gather at muddy puddles or on damp earth to drink. This activity is known as puddling. At dusk, most butterflies seek a safe place to roost (rest) for the night. Moths generally hide themselves away during the day. They conceal themselves against tree bark or under leaves so they cannot be seen by predators.

▲ **LAZY DAYS**
A day's undisturbed rest is important for night-flying moths such as this Sussex Emerald. It rests on or under leaves with its green wings outstretched, well disguised amongst the vegetation. Most other Geometer moths rest in this position during the day too, on leaves or against tree bark. Before flight, they shiver to warm up their wings.

▲ **DRY PUDDLING**
A Malayan butterfly sucks up mineral-rich water from sand through its proboscis (tongue). Some species of butterfly do not need a puddle in order to go puddling. In some dry regions, the male butterfly may be able to get the sodium salts it needs by spitting on and sucking dry stones, gravel or even the dried carcasses of animals.

▲ **SALT SEEKERS**
Puddling is a common activity in warm regions. However it is not a communal activity. In some regions butterflies and moths puddle on their own. Although they appear to be drinking, only males seem to puddle like this. It is believed that they absorb important salts dissolved in the water. Sodium salts are needed to produce the sperm packets passed on to females during mating.

▶ BASKING ON LICHEN

A Small Tortoiseshell butterfly (*Aglais urticae*) basks in a park on a carpet of lichen. It rests with its wings open wide and flat, to soak up the sun's warmth. The Small Tortoiseshell lives in cooler parts of the world, in Europe, Siberia and Japan. It therefore needs to bask in the sunshine to warm up its wing muscles before flight.

Did you know? The Grayling butterfly tilts to one side while resting to reduce the shadow cast by its wings.

Black-veined White butterfly
(*Aporia crataegi*)

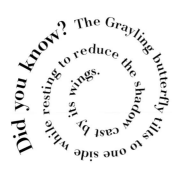

▲ SUN LOVERS

The Marbled White and other members of the Satyridae family have an unusual way of holding their wings when basking. They are held in a V-shape instead of fully opened or folded upright. The white of their wings reflects sunlight on to their abdomens.

▲ ROOSTING IN THE RAIN

Most butterflies escape the worst of the rain by roosting under leaves, but some of them stay out in the open. With their wings tightly closed, like this Black-veined White, the rain just runs over their scales and drips off. The wings dry almost immediately when the sun comes out.

163

Focus on

Skippers are not closely related to other butterflies. Most are less than 40mm across, with swept-back wings that make them highly agile. Skippers beat their wings rapidly and can change direction suddenly in mid-air, quite unlike other butterflies. The name Skipper refers to this darting, dancing flight. More than 3,000 species exist worldwide, including about 40 in Europe and 300 or more in North America. Most Skippers are brown or orange, but some tropical species, such as the Peruvian Skipper, have brilliant colours.

SHAPES

The body of this rainforest butterfly (*Haemactis sanguinalis*) is typical of all Skippers. It has a plump, hairy body that is more like a moth's than a butterfly's. The tips of their antennae are hooked not clubbed like other butterflies.

CIGAR CATERPILLARS

Skipper caterpillars are shaped like smooth cigars. They have distinct necks and their heads are usually different in colour from the rest of their bodies. They normally live in shelters made of leaves and spun silk.

Skippers

NIGHT-FLYING SKIPPER

This Peruvian Skipper is not as drab and moth-like as many Skippers but, like moths, it flies at night. It flies with a whirring sound produced by its wing beats. This is another feature Skippers share with moths.

TRINIDAD SKIPPERS

Most skippers in Europe and North America are dull shades of brown and many resemble moths more than butterflies. However, many tropical species are more brightly coloured, including this pair from Trinidad in the West Indies.

THISTLE FEEDER

The Silver-spotted Skipper haunts chalk hills and flies close to the ground. It likes to roost and feed on the flowers of low-growing thistles. Although it basks like the Large Skipper (*right*), it shuts its wings in dull weather.

GOLDEN SKIPPERS

The Large Skipper, seen here on knapweed, is a member of a group called Golden Skippers. They bask in an unusual way, flattening their hindwings and tilting their forewings forward. Male Golden Skippers have scent scales in a black streak in the middle of their wing.

Migration

Some butterflies and moths live and die within a very small area, never moving far from their birthplace. However, a few species are regular migrants. They are able to travel astonishing distances in search of new plant growth, or to escape cold or overpopulated areas. Some butterflies are truly worldwide migrants in a similar way to migratory birds. Every now and then small swarms of North American butterflies turn up in Europe after crossing the Atlantic Ocean. Crimson-speckled moths have been spotted thousands of kilometres out over the Southern Atlantic. Nevertheless, butterflies are unlike birds in that most only migrate one way and do not return to their original homes.

Canada

Atlantic Ocean

Pacific Ocean

USA

Mexico

Central America

Migration path

▲ MONARCH ROUTES
Monarch butterflies *(Danaus plexippus)* migrate mainly between North and Central America. A few have crossed the Atlantic and settled on islands off Africa and Portugal. Others have flown all the way to Ireland.

▲ MONARCH MASSES
Every autumn huge numbers of Monarchs leave eastern and western North America and fly south. They spend the winter in Florida, California and Mexico on the same trees settled by their grandparents the previous year.

▲ KING OF MIGRANTS
In March, Monarch butterflies journey over 3000km northwards, lay their eggs on the way and die. When the eggs hatch the cycle begins again. The month-old butterflies either continue north or return south, depending on the season.

◀ AN AFRICAN MIGRANT

This Brown-veined White butterfly has large wings capable of carrying it over long distances. Millions of these butterflies form swarms in many parts of southern Africa. A swarm can cause chaos to people attempting to drive through it. Although this butterfly flies throughout the year, these swarms are seen most often in December and January.

Did you know? A large swarm of migrating butterflies can bring farm machines to a standstill by resting on them.

▶ HAWK MOTH

Every spring thousands of Oleander Hawk moths set off from their native tropical Africa and head north. A few of them reach the far north of Europe in late summer. Hawk moths are among the furthest flying of all moths. They are able to travel rapidly over long distances.

Oleander Hawk moth
(Daphnis nerii)

▲ HIBERNATING PEACOCK

The adult Peacock butterfly sleeps during the winter. This sleep is called hibernation. The Peacock is protected by chemicals called glycols that stop its body fluids from freezing. Many other butterflies and moths survive the winter in this way instead of migrating.

▶ PAINTED LADY

The Painted Lady butterfly *(Vanessa cardui)* migrates almost all over the world. In summer it is found across Europe, as far as north as Iceland. However, it cannot survive the winter frosts. Adults emerging in late summer head south, and a few reach North Africa before the autumn chill starts.

167

Enemies and Disease

Many butterflies and moths lay huge numbers of eggs. Sometimes a single female can lay more than a thousand at any one time. However, these eggs are attacked by predators, parasites and disease from the moment they are laid. Caterpillars and adults also have many enemies and are preyed on by creatures such as birds, bats, lizards, spiders, hornets, and beetles. They are also attacked by parasitic wasps and flies that lay eggs inside caterpillars' bodies. Those that survive the attack of these predators and parasites may fall victim to diseases or harmful fungi.

▲ **DEADLY BIRDS**
Birds are the most dangerous enemies of butterflies and moths. Many types of bird prey upon adult insects. In spring, birds such as blue tits are often seen flying back to their nests with beakfuls of fat, juicy caterpillars for their young.

▲ **BAT ATTACK**
An Eyed Hawk moth is devoured by a Serotine Bat, leaving only wings and eggs. Night-flying moths often fall victim to bats, who can track them down in pitch darkness.

▲ **PROWLING FOXES**
Foxes seem unlikely predators of caterpillars. Surprisingly, though, when scientists have examined the stomach contents of dead foxes, they have found huge quantities of caterpillars. Foxes are sometimes forced to eat caterpillars when other food is scarce.

▶ UNWELCOME GUESTS

An Eyed Hawk moth caterpillar is killed by parasitic flies of the Tachinidae family. Many caterpillars are killed in this way. The fly injects its eggs into the caterpillar's body, and the newly hatched grubs eat away the body from the inside. The grubs grow and eventually bore their way out.

Gatekeeper butterfly
(Pyronia tithonus)

Clump of red mites.

◀ RED MITES

The red blob on the back of this Gatekeeper butterfly is a clump of red mites. These mites are larvae that cling on to butterflies of the Satyridae family. They feed on the butterfly's blood until they are full and then drop off, apparently doing the butterfly little harm.

Crab spider with its fangs in an unsuspecting victim.

▶ POUNCING SPIDERS

A butterfly that is sitting motionless on a flower for a long time may not be resting. It may have been killed by a crab spider. Creamy yellow crab spiders blend in so well on flower heads that many butterflies do not notice them and fall victim to their deadly venom.

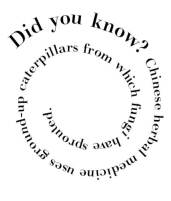

Did you know? Chinese herbal medicine uses ground-up caterpillars from which fungi have sprouted.

European Map butterfly
(Araschnia levana)

169

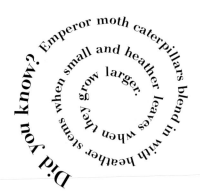

◀ **PUPA PROTECTION**

A Citrus Swallowtail pupa mimics a curled-up green leaf. Pupae remain motionless for weeks and are highly vulnerable, so camouflage is often their only protection.

Camouflage

Citrus Swallowtail butterfly pupa (Papilio demodocus)

Caterpillars and adult butterflies and moths are so vulnerable to attack that many have become masters of disguise. They hide from prying eyes by taking on the colours of trees, leaves and rocks. This defence is known as camouflage. Many moths fold back their wings during the day so they look like a leaf or a piece of bark. Most caterpillars are green to mimic leaves and grass or brown to mimic bark and mud. Inchworms (the caterpillars of Looper moths) are coloured and shaped to look just like twigs and even cling to stems at a twiglike angle.

Did you know? Emperor moth caterpillars blend in with heather leaves when small and heather stems when they grow larger.

▼ **LEAF MIMIC**

A wing of the Brazilian butterfly *Zaretis itis* looks like a dead leaf. The wing even mimics a leaf's natural tears and the spots made on it by fungi.

▲ **LYING LOW**

Geometrid moths are not easy to spot amongst dead leaves on the floor of a rainforest in Costa Rica. Another Costa Rican moth disguises itself as lichen. Moths rest in broad daylight, so they need to be especially well camouflaged.

Zaretis itis

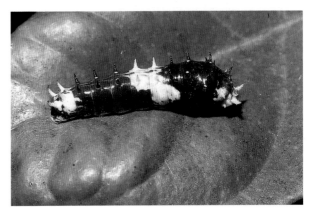

▲ HIDDEN LARVA

The caterpillar of the Orchard Swallowtail is camouflaged as a bird-dropping. Other caterpillars are brown or green, so they blend in with vegetation.

▲ FOLIAGE FRIENDLY

A Brimstone butterfly camouflages itself as a leaf by folding up its wings so that only the green underside is visible. The upper side of this butterfly's wings are the colour of brimstone (bright yellow), which is how the insect got its name.

Did you know? The moth Belenoptera sanguine rests with the front of its wings rolled up to resemble a leaf stalk.

▲ PINE MIMIC

The Pine Hawk moth (*Hyloicus pinastri*) is perfectly adapted to the pine forests in which it lives. Its mottled silvery-grey wings match the bark of pine trees. The moth is almost impossible to spot when it roosts during the day. Other moths imitate the bark of different trees.

▶ TWIGS

The Peppered moth caterpillar resembles a twig. It even has warts on its body like the buds on a twig. In the 1800s, a darker form of the adult moth became more common. This was because the soot from factories made tree trunks sooty. The darker moth blended in better on the dark trunks.

Peppered moth caterpillar
(*Biston betularia*)

Spotted Tiger moth
(Rhypasia purpurava)

Decoys and Displays

Camouflage helps to keep resting moths and butterflies hidden from the eyes of predators, but as soon as they move they become visible. Therefore butterflies and moths that fly during daylight hours must adopt other strategies to escape. The upper wings of many butterflies are coloured in all kinds of surprising ways to fool predators. Some mimic dangerous creatures. For example, the striped body, transparent wings and buzzing flight of a Hornet Clearwing moth make it resemble a stinging wasp from a distance. Others use colours or their wing shapes to confuse their predators. False antennae and eyes fool them into attacking from the wrong direction.

▲ CONFUSION

A Spotted Tiger moth escapes predators by surprising them with a quick flash of its brightly coloured underwings. When the moth is resting, these wings are hidden beneath its yellow forewings. A sudden flash of colour is often enough to confuse an enemy.

▶ BIG EYES

A Japanese Owl moth (*Brahmaea japonica*) flashes giant spots at a foe when threatened. These spots look like the staring eyes of a big owl, which scares off birds, lizards and other predators. Other moths display bright parts of their wings while in flight. When they are being chased, the predator focuses on the moth's bright wing. However, as soon as the moth lands the colour is hidden and the predator is confused.

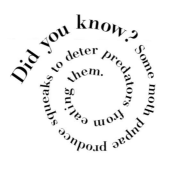

▲ TRICK OF THE EYE

Eyed Hawk moths have big eye spots on their hindwings. When in danger, the moth startles its enemy by flinging its wings open to reveal the enormous false eyes beneath.

Eye spots are hidden by forewings.

▶ SHUT EYES

A mating pair of Eyed Hawk moths hide their eye spots beneath their forewings. The effectiveness of eye spots depends on flashing them suddenly. To an inquisitive predator, it looks just like a cat or an owl opening its eyes – and the bird is frightened away.

Did you know? Some moth pupae produce squeaks to deter predators from eating them.

▶ TWO HEADS ARE BETTER THAN ONE...

This blue butterfly's secret escape system is the false eyes and mock antennae on its rear end. Predatory birds are fooled into lunging for the flimsy false head rather than the butterfly's real head at the other end. The butterfly then slips away from the bird's beak.

False eyes and antennae.

▲ WASP IMPERSONATOR

The Hornet Clearwing moth loses most of the scales from its wings on its first flight and then looks just like a wasp. Birds fear it has a vicious sting, although it is harmless.

▼ DECOY EYES

A Little Wood Satyr has false eyes at the edges of its wings. A huge number of butterflies and moths have similar spots on their wings. Birds peck at them, thinking they are real eyes. Butterflies are often seen flying with pieces bitten out of their wing edges. They do not seem to be troubled by having parts of their wings missing and are able to fly as normal.

173

Chemical Weapons

African Euchromia moth *(Euchromia lethe)*

Most butterflies and moths escape their enemies by avoiding being spotted. However, some use other tricks. They cannot sting or bite like bees or wasps, but many caterpillars have different ways of using toxic chemicals to poison their attackers, or at least make themselves unpleasant to taste or smell. For example, the caterpillar of the Brown-tail moth has barbed hairs tipped with a poison that can cause a severe skin rash even in humans. A Cinnabar moth cannot poison a predator, but it tastes foul if eaten. Usually, caterpillars that are unpalatable to predators are brightly coloured to let potential attackers know that they should be avoided.

▲ BRIGHT AND DEADLY

The brilliant colours of the African Euchromia moth warn any would-be predators that it is poisonous. It also has an awful smell. Some moths manufacture their own poisons, but others are toxic because their caterpillars eat poisonous plants. The poisons do not hurt the insects, but make them harmful to their enemies.

▲ HAIRY MOUTHFUL

The caterpillar of the Sycamore moth *(Apatele aceris)* is bright yellow. It is poisonous like some other brightly coloured caterpillars, but its masses of long, hairy tufts make it distinctly unpleasant to eat.

▼ THREATENING DISPLAY

The caterpillar of the Puss Moth may look as brightly coloured as a clown, but by caterpillar standards it is quite fearsome. When threatened, its slender whip-like tails are thrust forwards and it may squirt a jet of harmful formic acid from a gland near its mouth. It also uses red markings and false eye spots on its head to create an aggressive display.

Whip-like tail to threaten predators.

Puss Moth caterpillar *(Cerura vinula)*

◀ POISON MILK

A Monarch butterfly caterpillar feeds on various kinds of milkweed which contain a powerful poison. This chemical is harmful to many small creatures. The poison stays in the Monarch's body throughout its life. This may be why Monarchs show less fear of predators than other butterflies.

▶ RED ALERT

The striking red, white and black colours of the Spurge Hawk moth caterpillar announce that it is poisonous. Unpalatable insects frequently display conspicuous colours such as reds, yellows, blacks and white. These insects do not need to protect themselves by blending into their background. This caterpillar acquires its poison from a plant called spurge.

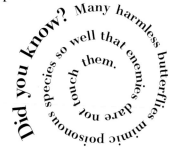

Spurge Hawk moth caterpillar
(Hyles euphorbiae)

Did you know? Many harmless butterflies mimic poisonous species so well that enemies dare not touch them.

▼ SMELLY CATERPILLARS

The Swallowtail caterpillar produces an odour that is strong enough to ward off parasites. It comes from a scent-gland called the osmeterium situated just behind its head. This gland suddenly erupts and oozes acid when the caterpillar is threatened.

▲ DEFENSIVE FROTH

Rhodogastria moths of Australasia often have a bright red abdomen to warn others that they carry a deadly poison. When the moth is threatened, this poison oozes as a green froth from a gland on the back of its neck.

Swallowtail caterpillar
(Papilio machaon)

Around the World

Butterflies and moths are surprisingly adaptable creatures. Almost every land mass in the world has its own particular range of butterfly and moth species. They inhabit a huge variety of different places, from the fringes of the hottest deserts to the icy wastes of the Arctic. Species are adapted to living in these very different environments. For example, butterflies and moths that live in cold areas tend to be darker than those that live in warm regions. This is because they need to be warm in order to fly and dark colours soak up sunlight more easily. In mountainous areas, the local species usually fly close to the ground. Flying any higher than this would create a risk of being blown away by the strong winds.

Orange-tip butterfly (*Anthocharis cardamines*)

◄ **MEADOWS AND WAYSIDES**
Farmland is an increasingly hostile habitat for butterflies. Intensive cultivation strips away wild flowers and grasses, while crop-spraying poisons the insects. However, many butterflies still thrive in meadows and hedgerows around the fields. Orange-tips, Meadow Browns, Gatekeepers, Small Coppers, Whites and Blues are still common, as are Noctuid and Geometrid moths.

Apollo butterfly (*Parnassius apollo*)

◄ **MOUNTAINS**
Butterflies that are adapted to life high on the mountains include the Alpine and Mountain Arguses and the Apollo. The Apollo's body is covered with fur to protect it from the extreme cold. Most Apollo eggs that are laid in autumn do not hatch until the following spring because of the low temperatures. Those caterpillars that do hatch hibernate at once.

◄ **MARSHES AND WETLANDS**
The Marsh Fritillary flourishes among the grasses and flowers of wetlands in temperate regions (areas that have warm summers and cold winters). Its caterpillar's favourite food plant is devil's bit scabious. Among the many other butterflies that thrive in wetlands are the Swallowtail, the White Peacock, and the Painted Skipper.

▶ DIFFERENT HABITATS

Butterflies and moths inhabit a wide range of regions. Species such as the Large White live in town gardens, while Graylings, Spanish Festoons and Two-tailed Pashas often live in coastal areas. Deserts are home to Painted Ladies, and White Admirals flutter about in woodland glades. Arctic species include the Pale Arctic and Clouded Yellow. Apollos and Cynthia's Fritillary are examples of Alpine types.

▼ GARDENS

All kinds of butterflies and moths visit gardens, including the Peacock *(Inachis io)*. Here they find an abundance of flowers to feed on – not only weeds, but also many garden flowers. Many of these flowers are actually related to wild hedgerow and field flowers such as buddleias, aubretias and Michaelmas daisies.

ALPINE · MARSHES · MEADOWS · URBAN · GARDENS AND GLADES · COASTAL · DESERT · ARCTIC MEADOW

The Warrior Symbol

A statue of a proud warrior stands at the ancient Toltec capital city of Tula in Mexico. An image of a butterfly appears on the warrior's breastplate. The Toltec people knew that butterflies live short but brilliant lives. Consequently, the butterfly became a symbol for Toltec soldiers who lived a brave life and did not fear death.

Indian Moon moth
(Actias selene)

Tropical Species

More species of butterfly and moth live in tropical parts of the world (regions near the Equator) than anywhere else. Tens of thousands of known species populate the tropical rainforests, and new species are being discovered almost every day. Some of the most spectacular and beautiful of all butterflies live in the tropics. These include shimmering Blue Morphos, vivid Orange Albatrosses, and exquisite Banded King Shoemakers. A large number of striking moths live in these areas, too, including the Indian and African Moon moths and the Golden Emperor.

▲ **MOONLIT MOTH**

The ghostly green-white wings of the Moon moth shine dimly on moonlit nights in forests ranging from Indonesia to India. Its huge wings measure 12cm in width and up to 18cm in length. The long tails, which are shaped like crescent moons, flutter in the shadows beneath the trees.

Painted Lady
(Vanessa cardui)

▲ **POSTMAN BUTTERFLY**

The brightly coloured Postman butterfly is found across a wide area of South America and has many different sub-species. These butterflies eat pollen as well as nectar.

▲ **DESERT WANDERER**

The Painted Lady butterfly lives in warm regions, although in summer it is often seen far to the north in Europe and North America. In autumn, it flies south to avoid perishing in the cold. In Africa, the natural homes of this species are the edges of the Sahara desert.

178

► EMERALD JEWEL

The Swallowtail family of butterflies (known by scientists as the Papilionids) includes some of the biggest and most beautiful of all butterflies. Among the most prized is the shimmering green *Papilio palinurus* that lives in the rainforests of South-east Asia. Its green colouring blends in perfectly with the lush vegetation. Many types of Swallowtail are protected species because of humans cutting down large areas of rainforest.

Green Swallowtail butterfly
(Papilio palinurus)

◄ METALMARK

A Metalmark (*Caria mantinea)* feeds on salts from damp ground. This butterfly is one of the Metalmark (or Riodinidae) family. It is one of the few families that are almost entirely restricted to the tropics. Their distinctive, rapid zigzag flight is often seen in rainforests.

Did you know? The Cattle Heart Swallowtail of Central and South America flies at heights of up to 1,500m along the edges of rainforests.

► WISE OWL

Owl butterflies, such as *Caligo memnon* of South and Central America, are some of the most distinctive of all tropical butterflies. Their large eyespots suggest the staring eyes of an owl. They feed mainly on bananas. For this reason, many owners of banana plantations regard these butterflies as pests.

Owl butterfly
(Caligo memnon)

Woodland Species

Purple hairstreak
(Quercusia quercus)

▲ **OAK EATER**

The Purple Hairstreak's favoured food plant is the oak tree. It can be found almost anywhere where large oaks grow in Africa and Asia. The adults do not seek out flowers for nectar because they flutter high in trees to feed on honeydew (a sweet liquid secreted by aphids).

Butterflies and moths have suffered from intensive farming in open country, but they still flourish in woodlands. A small number live in dense woods where there are few flowers. Larger numbers gather around clearings or glades. Certain species live mostly at low, shady levels while others prefer to dwell high among the treetops. The largest number of species live in mixed woodland, where food sources are varied. However, some species prefer particular kinds of woodland. For example, the Pine Hawk moth is common in coniferous forests, the Lobster moth is found in beech woods and the Green Oak Tortrix likes oak woodlands.

▲ **SHIMMERING PURPLE**

The Lesser Purple Emperor *(Apatura ilia)* and its cousin the Purple Emperor are among the most magnificent of all woodland butterflies. Their rapid, soaring flight is highly distinctive, as are their shimmering purple wings. They can often be seen near streams and ponds around willows, on which their caterpillars feed.

▲ **DEAD LEAF MOTH**

The Lappet moth is perfectly adapted to woodland life. When its wings are folded in rest it looks just like a dead leaf. Its caterpillar feeds on blackthorn, apple and other fruit trees, and is regarded as a pest by orchard owners.

Did you know? Pine White caterpillars can completely strip a pine tree of its needles.

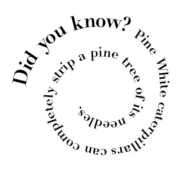

▶ FRITILLARY FLUTTER

The Silver-washed Fritillary is one of a large number of related species that inhabit woodlands. It can often be seen gliding through clearings and over woodland paths searching for nectar-rich bramble blossom. Its caterpillars feed on violet leaves.

Silver-washed Fritillary
(*Argynnis paphia*)

◀ OAK MOTH

The Oak Hooktip moth (*Drepana binaria*) lives in woodlands wherever there are oak trees. It flies mainly at night, but is sometimes seen on sunny afternoons. Its browny colouring blends perfectly with the bark on which it rests. Its caterpillar feeds on oak leaves. When it is fully grown it pupates inside a cocoon spun between two oak leaves.

The Legend of Etain

An old Irish myth tells of Etain, who became a butterfly. At first, he was changed into a puddle by his first wife, who was jealous when he remarried. A worm was born from the puddle. This turned into a beautiful butterfly which was sheltered and guarded by the gods.

▲ SPOTS AND STREAKS

The Brindled Beauty gets its name from the feathery bands on its wings. The word brindled means marked with spots or streaks. As well as living in woods, it is common in parks and gardens. Its caterpillars eat the leaves of various trees.

Focus on

1 Hawk moths begin life as eggs laid on the leaves of the food-plant. The round eggs are a distinctive shiny green. They are laid singly or in small batches and hatch a week or two afterwards.

2 The Elephant Hawk moth's name comes from the ability of its caterpillar to stretch out its front segments like an elephant's trunk. It takes about six weeks to grow fully and, like most hawk moths, it passes the winter in the pupal stage.

Hawk moths are perhaps the most distinctive of all the moth families. Their scientific name is *Sphingidae*. Their bodies are unusually large and they are strong fliers. Hawk moths can fly at speeds of up to 50km an hour, and many hover like a hummingbird while feeding from flowers. Many hawk moths have very long tongues that enable them to sip nectar from even the deepest flowers. When these moths come to rest, their wings usually angle back like the wings of a jet plane. Hawk moth caterpillars nearly all have a pointed horn on the end of their bodies.

3 The adult Elephant Hawk moth is one of the prettiest of all moths. It flies for a few weeks in the summer. Its candy-pink wings are a perfect match for the pink garden fuchsias and wild willow-herbs on which it lays its eggs.

Hawk Moths

POPLAR HAWK MOTHS

During the late spring and summer, Poplar hawk moths can often be seen flying towards lighted shop windows in European towns at night. They have a short tongue and do not feed. Unusually for hawk moths, when they are resting during the day, their hindwings are pushed in front of the forewings.

Poplar hawk moth
(Laothoe populi)

HONEY LOVER

The Death's Head Hawk moth *(Acherontia atropos)* is named after the skull-like markings near the back of its head. Its proboscis is too short to sip nectar. Instead, it sometimes enters beehives and sucks honey from the combs.

MASTER OF DISGUISE

The Broad-bordered Bee Hawk moth *(Hemaris fuciformis)* resembles a bumblebee. It has a fat, brown and yellow body and clear, glassy wings. This helps protect it from predators as it flies during the day.

Superfamilies

Scientists group butterflies and moths into 24 groups known as superfamilies. All but two of these superfamilies are moths, ranging from the tiny Micropterigoidea to the huge Bombycoidea. This latter group contains the giant Atlas moths. Butterflies belong to the other two superfamilies. The first, Hesperoidea, includes all 3,000 or so species of Skippers. The second, Papilionoidea, consists of about 15,000 species, divided among several families. These families include Papilionidae (Swallowtails, Apollos and Festoons), Pieridae (Whites and Yellows), Lycaenidae (Blues, Coppers and Hairstreaks) and Nymphalidae (Fritillaries, Morphos, Monarchs, Browns and Satyrs).

▲ **FEATHERY FAMILY**
The Plume moths (Pterophoridae) are small but very distinctive. They get their name from the way their wings are branched in feathery fronds, making them look almost like craneflies.

European Swallowtail butterfly (*Papilio machaon*)

Garden Tiger moth (*Arctia caja*)

◄ **ARCTIIDAE**
Tiger moths belong to a family of moths called the Arctiidae. Many of them are protected from predators by highly distasteful body fluids and a coat of irritating hairs, which they announce with their striking colours and bold patterns.

▲ **GREAT BEAUTIES**
Swallowtail butterflies belong to a family called Papilionidae. This family contains about 600 species. It includes some of the largest and most beautiful of all butterflies, such as the Birdwings of South-east Asia and the African Giant Swallowtail, whose large wings reach about 25cm across.

◄ THE BRUSH-FOOTS

The Fritillaries belong to one of the largest families of butterflies, called the Nymphalidae. This family is sometimes known as the brush-foots, because their front legs are short and covered in tufts of hair. The Fritillaries get their name from *fritillaria*, the ancient Roman game of chequers.

▼ AN EXCLUSIVE BUNCH

The Japanese Oak Silk moth has brown wing markings, unlike the famous white Silk moth of China. Silk moths belong to a family of moths called the Bombycidae. Only 300 species of Bombycidae are known to exist. Silk moths are among the best known of all moths because of the ability of their caterpillars to spin large quantities of silk.

Japanese Oak Silk moth
(Antheraea pernyi)

This moth possesses distinctive clear windows in its wings.

▲ TROPICAL RELATIVES

The beautiful and aptly named Glasswing butterfly of South America is a member of a group called the Ithomiids. This group forms part of the larger Nymphalidae (or brush-foot) family, which are found all over the world. Ithomiids, however, live only in the tropics.

► SMALL WONDERS

The Longhorn moths belong to a family of tiny moths called the Incurvariidae. These European moths are often metallic in colour. Longhorn moths are easily recognised by their unusually long antennae.

Conservation

Ever-increasing numbers of butterfly and moth species are becoming rare or even endangered. Their homes are lost when forests are cut down, hedgerows pulled up, wetlands drained and fields sprayed with pesticides. All wild creatures have been endangered to some extent by human activity, but butterflies and moths have suffered more than most. The life of each species is dependent on a particular range of food plants. Any change in the habitat that damages food plants can threaten butterflies and moths. For example, the ploughing up of natural grassland has significantly reduced the numbers of Regal Fritillary in North America, while tourism in mountain areas may kill off the magnificent Apollo butterfly.

▲ **MORPHO JEWELLERY**
Millions of brilliant Blue Morpho butterflies are collected and made into jewellery. Only the brightly coloured males are collected, leaving the less colourful females to lay their eggs.

▼ **AT RISK**
The False Ringlet is probably Europe's most endangered butterfly. The drainage of its damp grassland habitats has led to its disappearance from all but a few areas.

False Ringlet
(*Coenonympha oedippus*)

▲ **FATAL COLLECTIONS?**
In the 1800s, millions of butterflies were caught and killed by collectors. However, their activities had little effect on populations, because each adult female lays more than enough eggs to make up the difference. However, the destruction of their habitats in the 1900s has now made some species so rare that collecting even a few specimens may tip the balance against their survival.

Did you know? A butterfly collector once painted eyespots on the wings of a common species to pretend it was a new species.

▼ PRIZED SWALLOWTAIL

The stunning Scarlet Swallowtail butterfly is found only in the Philippines. It is now under threat as its rainforest habitat is destroyed by urban development. Thoughtless collectors also trap this insect as a highly prized specimen.

▲ SLASH AND BURN

Rainforests are burned away by developers to create new farmland and towns. Many species of butterfly and moth are threatened by the destruction of their habitat.

Scarlet Swallowtail butterfly
(Papilio rumanzovia)

▲ PUSHED OUT

The Kentish Glory *(Endromis versicolora)* moth became extinct in England in the 1960s. This was when the birchwoods in which it lived were destroyed.

ANCIENT MEXICO

The ancient civilizations of Mexico were fascinated by the many brilliant butterflies that inhabit this part of the world. The people of Teotihuacan (around 150BC – AD650) adorned some of their temples with butterfly carvings. The Aztecs (around AD1200 – 1525) also worshipped a butterfly god.

187

SOCIAL INSECTS

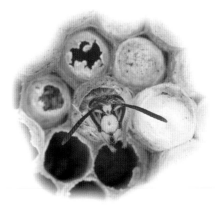

Most insects leave their young to fend for themselves, but a few care for their young in complex societies that are like miniature cities. All ants and termites, some types of bees and a few kinds of wasps are social insects. The insects in a colony share out the work of building and maintaining the nest, gathering food and caring for the young. Within each colony of insects, one or more females called queens lay eggs, workers (and sometimes soldiers) care for the young and defend the colony, while males mate with queens so they can lay more eggs. The largest colonies are those of termites, which may contain up to five million individuals.

What are Social Insects?

Insects are the most successful group of animals on Earth. They make up about three-quarters of all animal species. Most insects have a solitary life, but a few kinds are called social insects because they live and work together in a group known as a colony. Some insect colonies hold hundreds, thousands or even millions of insects. Different members of the colony do different jobs. All ants and termites, some types of bees and a few kinds of wasps are social. For centuries, people have been fascinated by these insects because their colonies seem similar to human societies. Some types of social insects are also important because they make useful products such as honey, and they help to pollinate flowers. For these reasons, social insects are among the world's best-known insect groups.

▲ LONELY LIVES

Most insects, such as these tortoiseshell butterflies, do not live in colonies. They spend almost all of their lives on their own. After mating, the female lays her eggs on a plant that will feed her young when they hatch. Then she flies away, leaving her young to fend for themselves.

▲ ONE LARGE FAMILY

This scene inside a honeybee's nest shows a fertile (breeding) female bee, called the queen, in the centre, surrounded by her children, who are called workers. Social insect colonies are like overgrown families. Each colony is made up of a parent or parents and lots of their offspring, who help to bring up more young.

Royal Emblem

This stained-glass window from Gloucester Cathedral, England, shows a fleur-de-lys, the emblem of the French royal family. 'Fleur-de-lys' is a French term for an iris or lily flower. Originally, however, the symbol represented a flying bee with outstretched wings. French kings chose the bee as their symbol because bee colonies function like well-run, hard-working human societies. Bees also represented riches because they made precious honey.

◀ TEAMWORK

These green tree ant workers are pulling leaves together to make a nest to protect the colony's young. Like all adult insect workers in a colony, they help rear the young but do not breed themselves. One ant working alone would not be strong enough to pull the leaf together – the task needs a group of ants working as a team.

DIFFERENT JOBS ▶

These two different types of termites are from the same species. The brown insects with large heads and fierce jaws are soldiers. They are guarding the smaller, paler workers, who are repairing damage to the nest. The insects in all social insect colonies are divided into groups called castes. Different castes have different roles, for example, worker termites search for food, while soldiers guard the nest. In some species, the castes look quite different from each other because they have certain features, such as large jaws, that help them do their work.

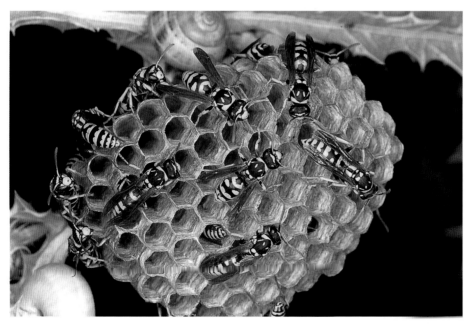

◀ NEST BUILDERS

Paper wasps are so called because they build nests made of chewed wood fibres or 'paper'. Like these wasps, most social insects live and rear their young inside a nest built by colony members. Some nests are complicated, beautiful structures, such as those made by some wasps and bees. Some nests, such as those made by certain termites, are huge in size and tower several metres high

Busy Bees

The insect world contains over a million different species (kinds) of insects. Scientists divide them into large groups called orders. All the insects in an order share certain characteristics. Bees belong to the order Hymenoptera. The name means 'transparent (see-through) wings', which bees have. Bees are found in most parts of the world except very cold places and tiny ocean islands. Experts have identified 20,000 different bee species. Many types live alone for most of the year, but over 500 species are social. They include honeybees, bumblebees and stingless bees. Honeybees live in colonies larger than those of any other bee.

▲ TINY BEES
This stingless bee is among the world's smallest bees – it is just 2mm long. Stingless bees live in hot, tropical countries near the Equator. These bees cannot sting, hence their name.

Common white-tailed bumblebee
(*Bombus lucorum*)

Worker

Drone

Queen

▲ HEAVYWEIGHT INSECT
Bees vary a lot in size. Bumblebees, such as the one shown here, are among the largest species. They grow up to 4cm long. Bumblebees are plump, hairy bees found in the Northern hemisphere in temperate regions. These bees live in small colonies where the queen has just a few workers to help her feed the young bees in the nest.

▲ IDENTITY PARADE
A honeybee colony contains three castes (types) of insect. The queen is the only fertile female. She lays all the eggs, and these hatch into the colony's young. Most of the other bees in the colony are females that do not breed. They are called workers. At certain times of year, male bees, called drones, hatch out. Their role is to mate with the queen so that she will lay more eggs.

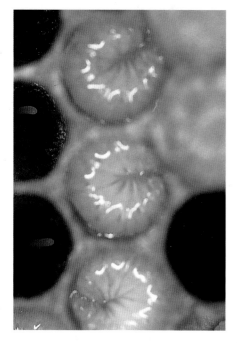

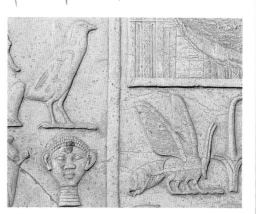

Bees in Ancient Egypt

This Egyptian tomb is carved with symbols of life, one of which is a large bee. The ancient Egyptians were among the first people to keep bees, over 2,500 years ago. They kept honeybees in clay hives, and even moved the hives from place to place in search of nectar-bearing flowers, in the same way some modern beekeepers do. Experts think the bees were probably transported by raft along the River Nile.

▲ SAFE NURSERY

These young honeybees are growing up in the nest, safe inside special cells that the worker bees have constructed. Wild bees usually build their nests in hollow trees or rocky crevices. People rear honeybees in artificial nests called hives, so that they can harvest the bees' honey to eat.

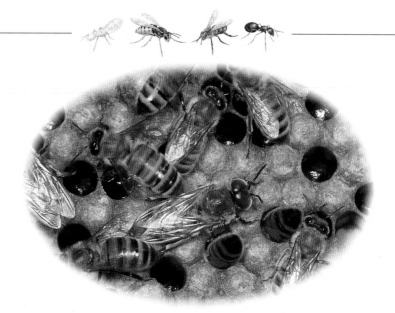

Brown bumblebee (*Bombus pascuorum*)

▲ DRONES AND WORKERS

These honeybees are male drones and smaller, female workers. The drones mate with the queen, while worker bees have many different tasks, such as looking after the young, making the nest larger and finding food.

◄ LONG-TONGUED BUMBLEBEE

This brown bumblebee is using her tongue to reach nectar deep inside the flower. Nectar is a sweet liquid made by flowers, which bees feed on. Back in the nest, the nectar is used to make honey. Brown bumblebees can be distinguished from other bumblebees by their unusually long tongues.

193

Hard-working Wasps

Bees and wasps are quite closely related. They belong to the same order, Hymenoptera. Like bees, wasps have transparent wings. Wasps live mainly in tropical or temperate regions, although a few species live in cold places. Experts have identified about 17,000 different species of wasps, but only about 1,500 species are social. They include common wasps, hornets and tree wasps. Social wasps live in nests that may contain as many as 5,000 insects. Most wasp nests contain only one fertile female, the queen.

▲ LARGEST WASPS

The weight of a queen hornet has caused this flower to drop a petal. European hornets, like the one above, are among the largest wasps, growing up to 2.5cm long.

▲ DISTINCTIVE STRIPES

These common wasp workers are entering their nest hole in a tree. Many types of wasps can be recognized by the bright stripes on their bodies. The colours warn other animals that the wasps are dangerous. Common wasps have yellow-and-black stripes.

CASTES OF THE COMMON WASP ▶

There are three castes (types) of wasps in a common wasps' nest – the queen, female workers (her daughters) and males (her sons). The queen is the largest wasp. Male wasps hatch out only in the breeding season.

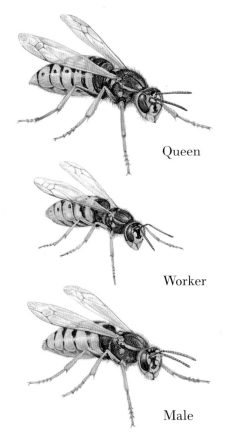

Queen

Worker

Male

◄ NEW WORKER

A paper wasp worker looks on as a younger sister, a new worker, hatches from the paper nest cell in which she has developed. Like other social insects, the nests of social wasps contain at least two generations of insects that work together to maintain colony life.

SWEET FEAST ►

Adult wasps like to feed on sweet foods such as fruit, plant sap and flower nectar. In autumn, you will often see common wasp workers gathering to feast on the flesh of ripe apples that have fallen to the ground.

◄ SLENDER NESTS

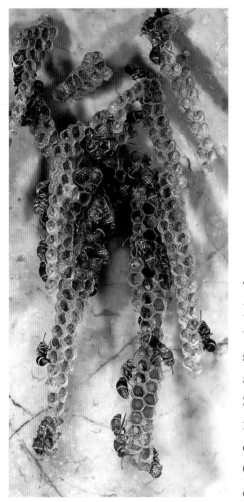

These Australian paper wasps have attached their nest to the roof of a dark cave. It is sheltered from the weather and from some predators. Some paper wasps build open nests in which the cells are clearly visible, as shown here. Others build a protective cover around their nests.

KEEPING COOL ►

This European paper wasp is removing water from her nest after a rainy night. In hot weather, the wasp cools her nest by sprinkling it with drops of water from a stream. Many types of wasps cool their nest by fanning it with their wings. European paper wasps often build open nests that hang from tree trunks.

195

Amazing Ants

The order Hymenoptera contains ants as well as wasps and bees. However, unlike their cousins, most ants do not have wings. Ants are found in many parts of the world, mostly in hot or warm countries. More than 9,000 different species of ants are found worldwide.

All types of ants are social. Some ant colonies are very large, and contain many thousands of individuals. Some ants nest high in trees, but most live underground. Ants are generally small in size. Most are about 1cm long, but some are only 1mm. Around the world, ants live in many amazing ways. Some species keep certain insects, such as aphids, captive and feed on the sweet food they produce. Other species keep other types of ants as slaves.

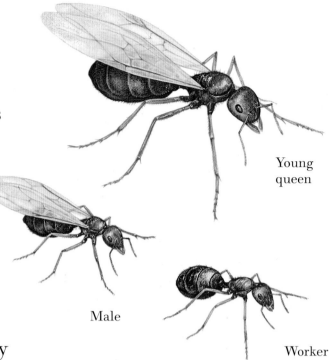

Young queen

Male

Worker

▲ ANT COLONY CASTES

Ant nests contain several different castes (types) of ants. There may be one or several queens, who have plump bodies. Male ants and young queens emerge during the breeding season – at this stage both have wings. Worker ants are smaller than the queen, and they perform many jobs around the nest. Some species of ant have a fourth caste of soldiers, whose job is to defend the colony.

▲ TINY BUT STRONG

This European wood ant is carrying a dead comrade to a rubbish tip outside the nest. Ants are very strong for their size. Some species can lift up to 50 times their weight.

FLYING HIGH ▶

Young queens and male ants have wings, and mate in the air. Afterwards, the male ant dies. The queen bites off her wings, as they are no longer needed. She digs into the soil to create a new nest. The queen rears the first brood of workers herself, feeding them on spare eggs and saliva.

▼ A FLYING SAUSAGE

The winged males of African safari ants have rosy, sausage-shaped bodies. They are known as sausage flies. Ants come in many colours, but the commonest colours are red or black.

African safari ant
(Dorylus helvolus)

▲ SCARY SOLDIER

An African driver ant soldier readies herself for action. Many species of ants have a special caste of soldiers that have large heads and fierce jaws. The soldiers' job is to protect the colony. African driver ants are particularly fierce. They usually prey on other insects, but sometimes attack much larger creatures such as birds and lizards, and domestic animals that have been tethered and can't escape. They work together to bring food back to the nest.

▲ SEWING A HOME

Weaver ant workers are holding the pale bodies of young ants, which are spinning silk. Weaver ants make their nests by joining leaves. The workers pull the leaves together, and then sew them with the silken threads.

FIGHT SCENE ▶

Some ants, such as these harvester ants, wage war on those from neighbouring colonies to gain possession of a good feeding area. Sometimes, an impressive show of strength is enough to force the rival ants to retreat.

197

Teeming Termites

Termites belong to the insect order Isoptera. The name means 'equal wings', even though most termites (the workers) do not have wings. Termites live mainly in tropical countries such as Africa and Australia, although some species are found in temperate parts of North and South America and Europe. All of the 2,000 species of termites are social.

Termites establish the largest insect colonies. A nest may contain up to five million individuals. Unlike other insect societies, a termite colony is made up of roughly equal numbers of males and females. As well as a queen, all termite colonies include a male called the king, who lives with the queen and fertilizes her eggs.

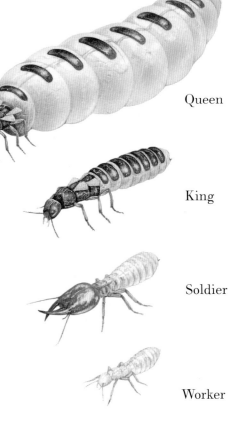

Queen

King

Soldier

Worker

▲ TERMITE CASTES

A termite colony contains four main castes (types) of insect – the queen, king, workers and soldiers. The queen is by far the largest insect in the colony, measuring up to 10cm long. The workers grow to only 5mm, a small fraction of her length.

▲ ROYAL FAMILY

This strange, sausage-shaped object is the termite queen. The rear part of her body is huge because it is swollen with thousands of eggs. Below her, to the right, you can see the king, who is a little larger than the workers. The king and queen normally live in a special chamber deep inside the nest.

▼ READY TO BREED

Termites emerge from their nest ready for their mating flight. After mating, the king and queen will found a new colony. They shed their wings and will probably remain underground for the rest of their lives.

▲ STRIPY SPECIES

The harvester termite worker has an unusual black-and-cream colouring. Its dark stripes help it to survive as it gathers plant food above the ground. Most termites live underground and find food there. They are pale-coloured and often die if exposed to bright sunlight for long.

▲ PALE INSECTS

This picture shows white, wingless termite workers and fertile (breeding) termites with wings. Most termites are pale in colour. For this reason, termites are sometimes called 'white ants', although they are not closely related to ants. All termite workers and soldiers are blind and wingless.

TALL TOWER ▶

An underground termite mound in Kenya is marked by a tower, which functions as a chimney. It contains ventilation shafts that allow cool air to reach the nest below. The tall spire, made by the tiny insects, may be as high as 7m. It is made of moistened mud that later dries rock-hard.

▲ WORKERS AND SOLDIERS

African termite workers gather grass and petals to feed the colony. They are guarded by soldiers, the large insects with well-armoured heads. Both soldier and worker termite castes contain male and female insects — roughly half of each.

Body Parts

Like all insects, adult social insects have six legs. Bees and wasps have wings, but non-breeding ants and termites (workers and soldiers) have no wings. As with other insects, the bodies of social insects are protected by a hard outer case that is called an exoskeleton. This tough covering is waterproof and helps to prevent the insect from drying out. An insect's body is divided into three main sections, the head, thorax (middle section) and abdomen (rear).

Social insects differ from non-social insects in some important ways. For example, they possess glands that produce special scents that help them communicate with one another. The various castes also have special features, such as stings.

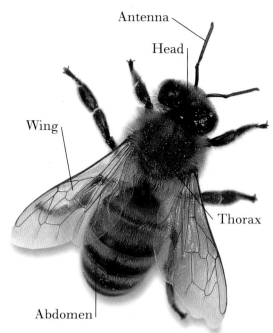

Antenna

Head

Wing

Thorax

Abdomen

▲ **PARTS OF AN INSECT**
An insect's head holds the main sense organs, including the eyes and antennae. Its wings, if it has any, and legs are attached to the thorax. The abdomen holds the digestive and reproductive parts.

Pollen-collecting hairs

▲ **BEE**
A bumblebee's body is covered with dense hairs. She collects flower pollen in special pollen baskets, surrounded by bristles, on her back legs.

▲ **WASP**
A wasp has narrow, delicate wings and a long body. In many wasp species, the abdomen and thorax are brightly striped.

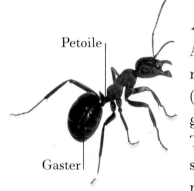

Petoile

Gaster

◀ **ANT**
An ant's abdomen is made up of the petoile (narrow waist) and the gaster (large rear part). The thorax contains strong muscles that move the six legs.

TERMITE ▶
Unlike other social insects, termites do not have a narrow 'waist' between their thorax and abdomen. They are less flexible than other social insects.

KEY

- ■ Respiratory system
- ■ Digestive system
- ■ Nervous system

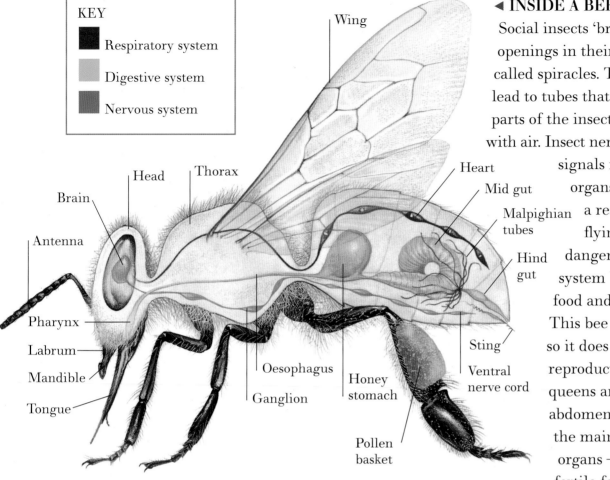

Wing

Head

Thorax

Brain

Antenna

Pharynx

Labrum

Mandible

Tongue

Oesophagus

Ganglion

Honey stomach

Pollen basket

Heart

Mid gut

Malpighian tubes

Hind gut

Sting

Ventral nerve cord

◄ INSIDE A BEE

Social insects 'breathe' through openings in their body case called spiracles. These holes lead to tubes that supply all parts of the insect's body with air. Insect nerves receive signals from the sense organs and organize a response, such as flying away from danger. The digestive system breaks down food and absorbs it. This bee is a worker, so it does not have any reproductive parts. In queens and males, the abdomen contains the main reproductive organs — ovaries for fertile females and testes for males.

Wasp Waist

In the late 19th century, it became fashionable for women to have a narrow 'wasp waist'. Well-to-do ladies achieved this shape by wearing corsets like the one shown in this advertisement. However, the corsets were very tight and pressed on the ribs and lungs. They were very uncomfortable and even caused some women to faint from lack of oxygen.

▲ COLD-BLOODED CREATURES

A queen wasp spends the winter in a sheltered place, such as a woodpile. Like all insects, social insects are cold-blooded, which means that when they are still, their body temperature is the same as the temperature outside. In winter, worker wasps die, but the queen enters a deep sleep called hibernation. She wakes up when the weather gets warmer again in spring.

On the Wing

All adult wasps and bees have two pairs of narrow, transparent (see-through) wings. They fly to escape their enemies and to get to food that cannot be reached from the ground. Honeybees fly off in swarms (groups) to start a new nest.

The wings of a bee or a wasp are attached to its thorax. Like other flying insects, bees and wasps may bask in the sun to warm their bodies before take-off. They also warm up by exercising their flight muscles. Flying uses up a lot of energy, so bees and wasps eat high-energy foods such as nectar. Most ants and termites are wingless, but young queens and males have wings, which they use during mating.

▲ **HOW BEES FLY**

Inside the thorax, bees and wasps have two sets of muscles that make their wings move. One set of muscles pulls down on the domed top of the thorax, which makes the wings flip up. Another set pulls on the ends of the thorax, so the top clicks back into its original shape. This makes the wings flip down.

▲ **BUZZING BEES**

A group of honeybees approaches a flower. Flying bees beat their wings amazingly quickly – at more than 200 beats per second. The beating movement produces a buzzing sound, which becomes more high pitched the faster the wings flap up and down.

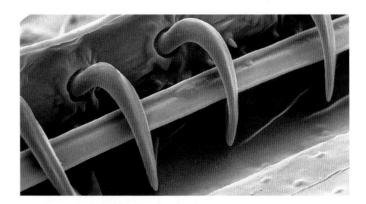

▲ **HOOKING UP**

This row of tiny hooks is on the edge of a bee's front wing. Wasps have wing hooks, too. The hooks attach the front wings to the hind ones when the insect is flying. Each wing has a larger surface area, helping the bee to move faster.

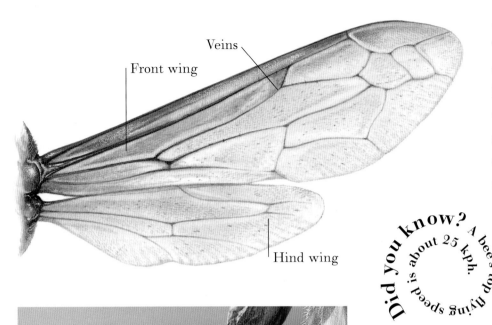

Front wing

Veins

Hind wing

◄ **DELICATE WINGS**

The front wings of bees and wasps are bigger than their hind (back) wings. The wings are made up of the same hard material, called chitin, that covers the rest of their body, but the wings are thin and delicate. They are supported and strengthened by a network of veins.

Did you know? A bee's top flying speed is about 25 kph.

French wasp (*Dolichivesoula media*)

▲ **SKILLFUL FLIER**

A brown bumblebee hovers in front of a flower. Bees are very agile in the air. They can move their wings backwards and forwards as well as up and down, so they can fly forward, reverse and also hover in one place.

▲ **KEEPING CLEAN**

This queen is cleaning her wings using tiny combs on her front legs. Bees and wasps clean their wings regularly to keep them in good working order. When not in use, they fold their wings over their backs to protect them from damage.

The Sound of a Bee

'Flight of the Bumblebee' is a piece of piano music that was written by the Russian composer Nikolai Andreyevich Rimsky-Korsakov (1844–1908). The piece was inspired by the buzzing sound that is made by these flying insects. The fast pace and quavering melody suggest the buzzing noise made by the bee as she moves from flower to flower, gathering nectar. The piece is well known for being very difficult to play.

Lively Legs

Most ants and termites cannot fly, but they move around and even climb trees using their six legs. Social insects also use their legs to groom (clean) their bodies.

All insects belong to a larger group of animals called arthropods, which means 'jointed leg'. True to this name, adult insects often have many-jointed legs. An insect's legs have four main sections — the coxa, femur, tibia and tarsus. The coxa is the top part of the leg, where it joins to the thorax. The femur corresponds to the thigh, and the tibia is the lower leg. The tarsus, or foot, is made up of several smaller sections. Insects' legs do not have bones. Instead, they are supported by hard outer cases, like hollow tubes.

Did you know? All adult insects have six legs, but young bees, wasps and ants have no legs at all.

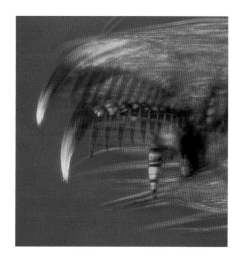

▲ **GRIPPING CLAWS**
This magnified photograph of a bee's foot shows clearly the tiny claws on the end of the foot. Claws help the insects to grip smooth surfaces such as shiny leaves, stems and branches without slipping. Ants can walk along the underside of leaves with the help of their claws.

WALKING ON STILTS ▶
Like other ants, this Australian bulldog ant has legs made up of several long, thin sections. In the hot, dry areas of Australia, the ant's stilt-like legs raise her high above the hot, dusty ground, helping to keep her cool. As well as walking, climbing and running, social insects' legs have other uses. Some ants and termites use their legs to dig underground burrows. Bees carry food using their hind legs.

▲ MULTI-PURPOSE LEGS

Bees use their legs to grip on to flowers and also to walk, carry nesting materials and clean their furry bodies. Their front legs have special notches to clean their antennae. They use their hind legs to carry pollen back to the nest.

▲ ON THE MOVE

Army ants spend their whole lives on the move. Instead of building permanent nests as other ants do, they march through the forest in search of prey, attacking any creature they find and scavanging from dead carcasses.

▼ EXPERT CLIMBERS

Termites swarm along a tree branch in Malaysia, South-east Asia. Many termites nest underground, but some build their nests high in trees. They climb vertical surfaces such as trees by digging their claws into the bark.

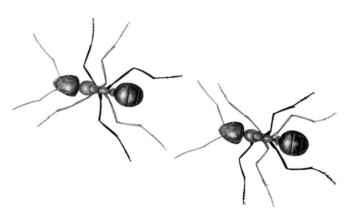

▲ THREE-LEGGED RACE

A running ant keeps three of her legs (shown in black) on the ground at the same time, but does not move all the legs on one side together. The front and hind legs touch the ground at the same time as the middle leg on the opposite side, helping to keep the ant steady.

Amazing Senses

Social insects find food, escape from danger and communicate with their nestmates with the help of their keen senses. However, the world their senses show them is very different from the one we humans know.

Antennae are the main sense organs for many insects. These long, thin projections on the insect's head are used to smell and feel, and sometimes to taste or hear. Sight is important to wasps, bees and most ants, but many termites have no eyes and are blind. Their world is a pattern of scents and tastes.

Social insects have no ears, so they cannot hear as people do. Instead, they 'hear' using special organs that pick up tiny air currents, or vibrations, produced by sounds. Sensitive hairs all over their bodies help the insects know when danger is near.

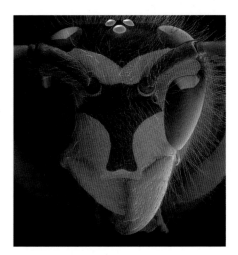

▲ **TWO TYPES OF EYE**
This close-up of a wasp shows the large compound eyes that cover much of the head. The curving shape of the eyes allows the wasp to see in front, behind and above at the same time. Compound eyes make out colours and shapes, and are good at detecting movement. On top of the wasp's head are three simple eyes, arranged in a triangle. These detect light and help the wasp know what time of day it is.

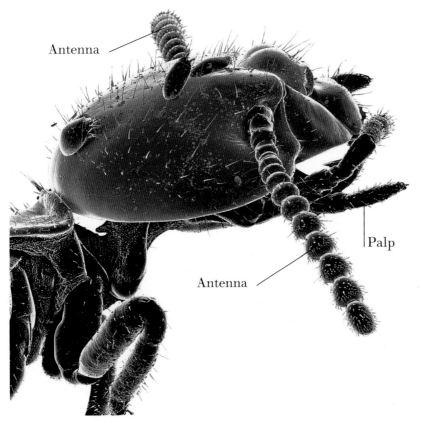

Antenna

Palp

Antenna

◀ **TOUCHY-FEELY**
This close-up of a soldier termite clearly shows its antennae – the main sense organs. They are divided into bead-like segments that are covered with tiny hairs, which send signals to the insect's brain. Shorter feelers called palps, on the mouth, give the termite a better sense of touch. The palps help it to find and guide food to its mouth. This termite has tiny parasites called mites crawling on its head.

▲ ELBOW ANTENNAE

A bull ant worker uses her feet to clean her antennae. Ant antennae have a sharp-angled 'elbow' joint, which can be seen here.

▲ BRISTLING WITH SENSES

Honeybee workers have compound eyes, simple eyes and short but sensitive antennae that pick up the scents of flowers. Hairs on the head detect wind speed and tell the bee how fast she is flying.

◄ MANY LENSES

A bee's compound eyes are made up of many small, six-sided lenses. Bees and wasps have thousands of these lenses in each eye. Some ants have only a few. Each lens lies at a slightly different angle from its neighbours on the curved surface of the eye, and each gives a slightly different picture. The insect's brain may combine all these little images to build up a big picture of the world.

Human's-eye view.

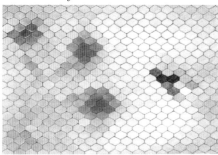

Possible bee's-eye view.

Did you know? Only the termite king and queen have eyes – workers and soldiers are blind.

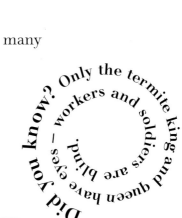

ON THE ALERT ►

Ants don't have ears so they use special organs on their antennae, body and feet to 'listen' out for prey. This Caribbean ant is lying in wait to pounce on passing minibeasts. It is in a special ambush position.

207

Armed and Deadly

Ants, bees, wasps and termites have many enemies in the animal kingdom but, unlike many insects, most social insects are armed. They use their weapons to defend the colony, and will often sacrifice their own lives in so doing. Bees and termites are armed for defence, but wasps and ants use their weapons to help kill or capture their prey.

Bees, wasps and some ants are armed with stings. Some ants and termites have powerful jaws that can deliver a nasty bite, while others can squirt a jet of poison at their enemies. Some wasps and bees have bright yellow-and-black or red-and-black markings on their bodies. These colour combinations, known as warning colours, tell other creatures that these insects are dangerous and best avoided.

▲ BARBED SPINES

A worker bee's sting has tiny barbs on the spine. These catch in the victim's flesh as the bee stings, so the bee cannot draw the sting out again. As the bee tries to free herself, part of her abdomen comes away with the sting, and she dies soon afterwards. Wasps and queen bees have smooth stings that they can pull out safely, so they don't die after they sting.

Did you know? Wasps and bees sting in self defence, so are unlikely to harm you unless you alarm them.

▲ NASTY STINGER

This close-up shows the sting of a common worker wasp. The sting of a wasp or bee consists of a sharp, hollow spine connected to a venom (poison) gland in the insect's abdomen. When the wasp or bee stings, the spine punctures its victim's skin, then the gland pumps venom into the wound. Only female wasps and bees have stings.

READY FOR ACTION ▶

Wood ants have powerful jaws that can give a painful nip. This cornered worker has taken up a defensive position with open jaws ready to bite. Her abdomen points upward, ready to spray acid from a poison gland in her abdomen. In this case, her enemy is the photographer who is taking the picture.

Wood ant
(*Formica rufa*)

▲ STINGING BEE

This honeybee is stinging a person's arm.
Bee stings cause pain and often produce
swelling. If you are stung by a bee, gently ease
the sting out, then wash the area with soap and
water. A cold, damp cloth can help to ease the
pain and bring down the swelling. The pain
lasts only a few minutes, but the swelling may
take a day or more to go down.

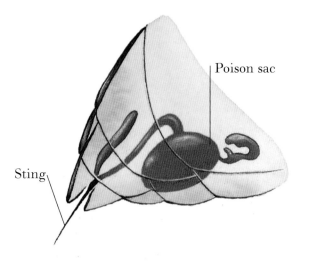

Poison sac

Sting

▲ INSIDE THE BODY

This diagram shows a wasp's sting, which
consists of a smooth, sharp spine, attached to a
poison gland in its rear end. If you are stung by
a wasp, wash the wound with antiseptic. Wasp
and bee stings are not life-threatening for
people, unless the victim is allergic to stings.

▲ A SOLDIER'S WEAPONS

A leafcutter soldier ant shows off its fierce jaws.
Many ants and termites can give their enemies
a nasty bite. Some types of termites have long,
nozzle-like snouts instead of large jaws. They
use the little nozzles to squirt a jet of sticky
poison at attackers to kill or immobilize them.

How Insects Eat

The mouthparts of insects are shaped to tackle the particular food they eat. Most social insects eat plant matter, but some species, such as army ants, eat meat and actively hunt their prey. Bees feed on sugary nectar and pollen from flowers. They also use nectar to make honey, which they eat in winter. Bee larvae are fed the same food as adults, but young wasps eat different food. Adult wasps feed mainly on liquid foods, but their larvae eat chewed-up insects.

Many ants eat liquid plant food. Some species lick sweet honeydew from aphids. Other ant species prey on caterpillars and worms, or even lizards, birds and mammals. Most termites and their young eat plant matter. They absorb the goodness in their food with the help of tiny organisms in their guts.

▲ NECTAR COLLECTOR
A honeybee's tongue forms a long, flexible tube that can be shortened or made longer and pointed in any direction. The worker bee uses her tongue like a drinking straw to suck up nectar. She stores most of the liquid in her honey stomach until she returns to the nest.

▲ DUAL-PURPOSE MOUTH
A common wasp laps up juice from an apple. Worker wasps have mouthparts designed to tackle both fluid and insect food. They slurp up liquid food for themselves with their sucking mouthparts, and use their strong jaws to chew up the bodies of insects for the young wasps in the nest.

◄ FEEDING TIME
A honeybee feeds another worker at the nest. As the bee laps flower nectar, strong muscles inside her mouth pump the sweet fluid into her honey stomach. Back at the nest, the worker regurgitates (brings up) the nectar to feed a nestmate, or stores the nectar in special larder cells.

▲ STRONG-JAWED ANT

A red carpenter ant shows her large, powerful, toothed jaws, called mandibles. An ant's jaws, which move from side to side, not up and down, are used to break off chunks of plant food.

▲ DAIRYING ANTS

These red ant workers are 'milking' black aphids for the sweet liquid called honeydew that the aphids give off as a waste product. Some types of ants keep the aphids like miniature cattle. They 'milk' their captives by stroking them with their antennae to get them to release the honeydew. The ants protect the aphids from their enemies, and in return, have a ready supply of food.

◄ WOOD-MUNCHERS

Termites feed mainly on soft, decaying wood in fallen trees and in human settlements. In tropical countries, they can damage wooden houses and destroy furniture, books and other wood products. They also cause great damage in plantations and orchards if they infest trees or crops.

HELP WITH DIGESTION ►

Inside a termite's body live even smaller creatures. These strange, pear-shaped forms are called protozoans and they live inside the guts of termites. This photo was taken using a microscope and has been magnified 65 times. Inside the termite's gut, the protozoans digest cellulose, a tough material that forms the solid framework of plants. In this way, the protozoans, and other tiny organisms called bacteria, help termites to break down and absorb the goodness in their food.

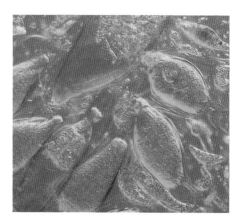

The Gardens of the

Leafcutter ants from Central and South America have rather unusual feeding habits. They live in underground nests where they grow their own food – a type of fungus (like tiny mushrooms). This particular fungus is found only in the ants' nests. The leafcutters tend them carefully in special chambers called fungus gardens. Leafcutter ants feed their fungi on bits of leaves that they snip from plants near the nest.

A leafcutter nest contains several types of workers that do different tasks. Some workers maintain the nest and feed and care for the queen and young, just as in most colonies. Other workers snip leaves and carry them back to the nest. Gardener ants prepare the leaf food for the fungi.

1 Leafcutter ants are so called because they snip off pieces of leaves with their sharp, pointed jaws. They use the leaf pieces to grow the special fungus that forms the ants' food. A huge quantity of vegetation is needed to keep the leafcutters' fungus gardens well supplied.

2 A line of leafcutter ants hoists the snipped leaves above their heads to carry them back to the nest. Leafcutter ants are also called parasol ants because the snipped leaves look like tiny parasols, or sunshades. The line of ants forms a small but spectacular parade as it makes its way back to the nest.

3 These leafcutter ant workers are large and strong enough to carry pieces of leaf many times their own size in their mandibles (jaws). In some leafcutter ant species, tiny ants called minors ride on the snipped leaves. They guard their larger worker sisters from flies that try to lay their eggs on the busy workers.

Leafcutter Ants

4 A line of leaf-carrying ants reaches the nest hole. There the leaf-bearers drop their loads for the gardener ants to deal with, and go back for more leaves. If heavy rain starts to fall, the ants drop their leaves and hurry to the nest site. Experts think they do this because a batch of soaking leaves would upset conditions inside the nest, and perhaps damage the growing fungi.

5 Gardener ants carefully tend the patches of fungi so that they will flourish. They snip up the leaves into smaller pieces and chew them up to form a compost for the fungi to grow in. They fertilize the compost with their droppings, and spread special chemicals that kill bacteria, which might harm the fungi. Other workers remove debris from the fungus gardens and keep them clean.

6 All leafcutter ants, including the queen (who is shown here) and her young, feed exclusively on the fungi. When a young queen leaves the nest to start a new colony, she carries a piece of fungus in her mouth, which she plants in her new nest. If the new colony flourishes it may one day hold a million workers. A large colony of leafcutter ant workers may shift up to 40 tonnes of soil as they excavate their vast underground nest.

Bee and Wasp Nests

Social bees and wasps build complex nests that house the queen, workers and young. Some of these insects nest underground, but many make their homes high in trees or caves, or under the eaves of houses.

Bee and wasp nests contain small six-sided brood cells where the young are reared. Some species also use the cells to store food. These little cells are often built in flattish sheets called combs. In warm countries, wasps and bees often build open-celled nests with no protective covering. In cooler countries, many species protect their nest by enclosing it in a tough covering. In the wild, honeybees construct nests with long, slender open-celled combs. They also live in human-made hives. Bumblebees live in smaller nests, often underground. Some tropical wasps build heavy mud nests hanging from a tree branch. These nests have a long, vertical slit-shaped opening.

▲ HOME SWEET HOME
Wild honeybees nest in tree holes. The slender combs are covered with cells made from wax. Workers have special glands on the underside of their abdomens to produce the wax.

HIDDEN NEST ►
Bumblebee queens make homes in abandoned animal burrows, rocky crevices or grassy hollows. The small nest contains an untidy comb with a few brood cells for the young. The queen also builds a little pot to store honey, which she feeds on in spring when she incubates her first batch of eggs. Bumblebee workers die off in winter, and only the young queens survive.

214

◄ BELL-SHAPED HOME

In Venezuela in South America, these tropical wasps have built a bell-shaped nest hanging from a tree branch. The nest looks heavy, but it is made of chewed wood fibres, and so is in fact fairly light.

▲ OUT OF HARM'S WAY

This long, slender wasp's nest in Central America is out of reach of many enemies. The nest is protected by a stout paper cover and has a small opening at the bottom. When threatened, some tropical wasps beat their wings on the nest case to make a loud sound that frightens enemies away.

CAMOUFLAGED AS A TWIG ►

In South America, some species of wasps build long, thin nests that resemble slender twigs hanging downwards, such as this one from Peru. Other South American wasps construct a paper nest with more prickles than a porcupine. Around the world, wasp nests vary in size as well as shape. The smallest are tiny, and the largest measure up to 1m long.

◄ NEST WITHIN A NEST

This skilful weaver bird in southern Africa is making its nest by tying grass into knots. The nest is hanging from a branch. Sometimes, a colony of *Philetarus* wasps will build their own home inside a weaver bird's nest. The wasps' brood cells are protected from the weather. In return, the stinging insects help to protect the birds from their enemies.

215

Ant and Termite Homes

Nests built by ants and termites come in many different shapes and sizes. Most build their colonies underground, but others live high in trees. Some ants' nests are tiny and contain only a small number of insects. They may be small enough to fit in tiny hollows in twigs or even inside the thorns of spiky plants. Other species live in vast underground colonies that shelter millions of workers and may cover an area the size of a tennis court.

Termites are master builders. Some species build vast underground homes with tall towers above ground that act as ventilation chimneys. These amazing structures allow cool air to flow through the living quarters of the colony, which keeps conditions comfortable there.

Did you know? Termites can control the temperature inside their nest to within 1°C.

▲ COSY FOREST HOME
In European woodlands, wood ants build large, domed nests of soil, twigs and pine needles. There may be a dozen separate mounds linked by a network of tunnels. In winter, the ants retreat to the deepest, warmest part of the nest. They move back into the upper chambers when the weather warms up again in spring.

◄ INSIDE AN ANTS' NEST
An ants' nest is a maze of narrow tunnels leading to wider living spaces called rooms or chambers. The queen lives and lays her eggs in a large chamber. The young ants are fed and reared in separate rooms called nurseries. Worker ants rest and gather in their own quarters. Other rooms are larders, where food is stored, or rubbish pits.

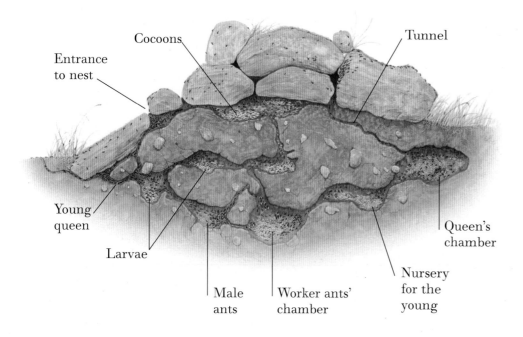

Cocoons
Entrance to nest
Tunnel
Young queen
Larvae
Male ants
Worker ants' chamber
Queen's chamber
Nursery for the young

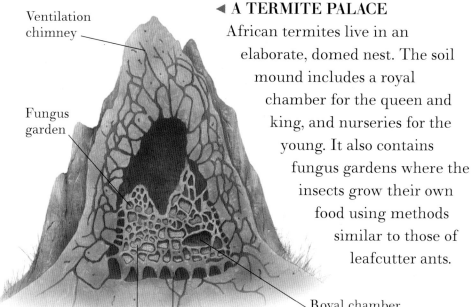

Ventilation chimney

Fungus garden

Nursery with eggs | Supporting pillar

Royal chamber housing king and queen

◄ **A TERMITE PALACE**
African termites live in an elaborate, domed nest. The soil mound includes a royal chamber for the queen and king, and nurseries for the young. It also contains fungus gardens where the insects grow their own food using methods similar to those of leafcutter ants.

▲ **MUSHROOM CAP**
Some termites from West Africa build mushroom-shaped mud chimneys. The shape helps the rain to run off easily. This chimney has been cut in half so you can see inside. It is full of tiny passages that the workers can open or block to adjust the temperature in the nest below. Up to five mushroom caps are sometimes stacked on top of one another.

TREE HOUSE ►
Most termites nest underground, but some species build treetop nests, such as this one in eastern Mexico. Nests on the ground are built of mud or sand. Tree nests are usually made from wood fibres moistened with the insects' saliva, a mixture that dries as hard as rock.

◄ **USING THE SUN**
Australian compass termites are so-called because they build nests with unusual, flat-sided chimneys that all face in the same direction, east–west. This allows the nest to be warmed by the weak rays of the sun at dawn and dusk. Only the narrow face of the chimney faces the fierce midday sun, which helps keep the nest cool.

217

Building a

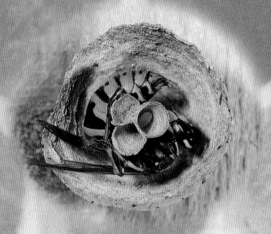

A Saxony wasp nest is started by the queen alone, without any help from her workers. The nest is made from chewed up wood fibres. It begins as a tiny cup and gradually grows to the size of a football or even larger. The gnawed fibres are soft and flexible at first, but later, dry hard and tough. While the nest is still small, the queen lays an egg in each cell on the comb. When the larvae (young insects) hatch, she feeds them on chewed-up insects. When her first brood become adult workers they take over the day-to-day running of the colony. As the numbers of insects in the colony grow, the nest gets bigger.

1 The Saxony wasp queen begins by making a little paper cup hanging from a strong support, such as a wooden beam. Like a tiny lampshade, the nest is suspended on a thin but flexible paper stalk. The queen builds cells for her first brood of young.

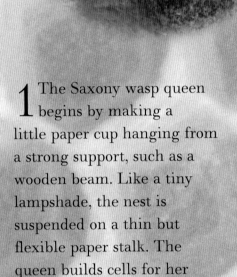

2 The queen collects fibres for her nest from an old fence post. She scrapes away small slivers of wood with her jaws, leaving little tell-tale grooves in the post. The rasping sound she makes with her jaws can be heard from some distance away. She has to make many trips to collect enough paper for the nest.

3 At night, the wasp queen sleeps coiled around the stem of her nest. You can see the brood cells hanging down inside the cup. Soon the queen will lay a tiny egg at the bottom of each cell. She glues the eggs firmly so they do not drop out.

Saxony Wasp Nest

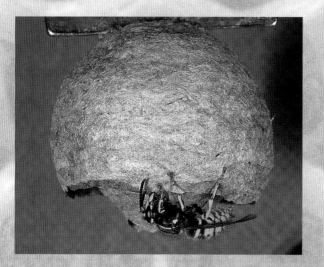

4 The queen builds a second paper 'envelope' around her nest to strengthen it. As the sides of the cup are extended downwards, the nest becomes more rounded. Eventually, only a small entry hole is left at the bottom so the wasps can enter and leave. Having a small opening makes the nest easier to defend.

5 The worker wasps now take over many tasks around the nest, including enlarging the nest. These workers are feeding the next batch of young. You can see the pale larvae curled up inside the open cells. Freed of her other duties, the queen is able to concentrate on laying eggs.

6 A worker improves the nest by adding a new layer to the outer covering. Inside, the old layers of envelope are gnawed away to make room for more brood cells. Towards the end of the season, young queens and male wasps hatch out and fly off to find mates. The queens will start new colonies the following year.

7 This abandoned Saxony wasp nest has been cut in half so you can see inside. The fully developed nest is the size of a football. Like a multistorey building, it contains many 'floors' of cells that are supported by paper pillars and connected by vertical passageways.

Bee and Wasp Colonies

Social bee and wasp colonies work like miniature, smooth-running cities. Like good citizens, all the insects in the colony instinctively know their roles and carry out their tasks.

In a honeybee colony, the workers perform different tasks according to their age. The youngest workers stay in the nest and spend their first weeks cleaning out the brood cells. Later they feed the young. As the wax glands in their abdomen develop, they help to build new cells. They also keep the nest at the right temperature. After about three weeks, the worker honeybees go outside to fetch nectar and pollen to store or to feed their sisters. The oldest, most-experienced workers act as guards and scouts. Many wasp colonies work in a similar way, with workers doing different jobs according to their age.

▲ ADJUSTING THE HEAT
Honeybees are very sensitive to tiny changes in temperature. The worker bees adjust the temperature around the brood cells to keep the air at a constant 34°C. In cold weather, they cluster together to keep the brood cells warm. In hot weather, they spread out to create cooling air channels.

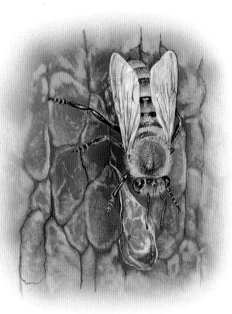

◄ NEST REPAIRS
Worker honeybees use a sticky tree resin to repair cracks in their nest. This gummy material is also known as propolis, or 'bee glue'. The bees carry it back to the nest in the pollen baskets on their hind legs. If there is no resin around, the bees may use tar from roads instead.

▲ BUILDING NEW CELLS
A worker honeybee builds cells using wax from her abdomen. She uses her antennae to check the dimensions of the cells because they must be exactly the right size.

◀ THREAT DISPLAY

Paper wasp workers from Equador in South America swarm over the outside of their nest to frighten off intruders. Like all wasp workers, one of their main roles is to defend the nest. If this display fails, the wasps will attack and sting their enemy. However, most animals will retreat as quickly as they can.

▲ PRECIOUS CARGO

A worker honeybee unloads her cargo of nectar. The bees use the nectar to make honey, which is a high-energy food. The honeybee workers eat the honey, which allows them to survive long, cold winters in temperate regions, when other worker bees and wasps die.

PROVIDING A MEAL ▶

A wasp worker feeds a larva (young wasp) on a ball of chewed-up insects. The young sister is allowed to feed for about ten seconds, then the worker remoulds the food ball and offers it to another larva. The adult may suck juices from the insect meat before offering it to the young. Up to four larvae can feed on the ball.

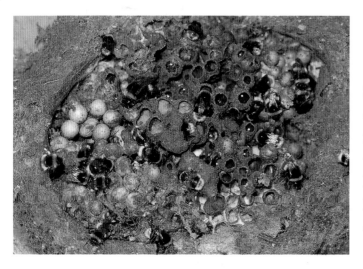

◀ LITTLE BUMBLEBEE NESTS

Social bumblebees live in much smaller colonies than honeybees. European bumblebee nests usually hold between 20–150 insects, whereas a thriving honeybee colony may hold 60–80,000 insects. The queen bumblebee helps her workers with the day-to-day running of the nest as well as laying eggs.

Ant and Termite Societies

Like bee and wasp societies, ant colonies are all-female for much of the year. Males appear only in the breeding season to mate with the young queens. Ant colonies are tended by hundreds or thousands of sterile female workers. The worker ants also fight off enemies when danger threatens, repair and expand the nest, and adjust conditions there. Some ants use the workers from other species as 'slaves' to carry out these chores.

In most types of ants, the large queen is still nimble and active. However, the termite queen develops a huge body and becomes immobile. She relies on her workers to feed and care for her, while she produces masses of eggs.

▲ **ON GUARD**
These ants are guarding the cocoons of queens and workers, who will soon emerge. One of the workers' main tasks is to defend the colony. If you disturb an ants' nest, the workers will rush out with the cocoons of young ants and carry them to a new, safe site.

▼ **RIVER OF ANTS**
Safari ants march through the forest in long lines called columns. The workers, carrying the cocoons of young ants, travel in the middle of the column, where it is safer. They are flanked by a line of soldiers on each side. Resembling a river of tiny bodies, the column may stretch more than 100m.

▲ **ANT RAIDERS**
Slavemaker ants survive by raiding. Here an ant is carrying off a worker from another species. Some slavemakers, such as red Amazon ants, have sharp, pointed jaws that are good for fighting, but no use for other tasks. They rely on ant slaves to gather food and run the nest.

◄ TERMITE SKYSCRAPER

These African termite workers are building a new ventilation chimney for their nest. African termites build the tallest towers of any species, up to 7.5m high. If humans were to build a structure of the same height relative to our body size, we would have to build skyscrapers that were more than 9.5km high. The tallest skyscraper today is less than 500m tall.

FAMILY LIFE ►

A queen termite is flanked by the king (the large insect below her), workers and young termites. The king and queen live much longer than the workers – for 15 years or even more in some species. The queen may lay 30,000 eggs in a day – that is one every few seconds. The king stays at her side in the royal chamber and fertilizes all the eggs.

Did you know? *A column of army ants on the march may contain 150,000 insects.*

A nasute termite (*Nasutitermes* species)

◄ BLIND GUARD

A soldier termite displays its huge head, which is packed with muscles to move the curved jaws at the front. Being blind, the guard detects danger mainly through scent, taste and touch. Like termite workers, soldiers may be either male or female, but they do not breed. The arch-enemies of these plant-eating insects are meat-eating ants, which hunt them for food.

223

Social Insect Habitats

Huge numbers of social insects live in tropical regions, where the climate is hot all year round. They include most termites and many different types of ants, wasps and bees. Rainforests are home to a greater variety of insects, including social species, than any other habitat on Earth. Many termite species live in dry grasslands, or savannas. Scrublands on the edges of deserts are home to some hardy social insects, such as honeypot ants. The world's temperate regions have warm summers and mild or coolish winters. They provide many different habitats, which are home to particular kinds of social insects. The polar regions are generally too cold for insects to survive.

▲ FOREST BIVOUAC
Driver ants spend their lives on the move through the South American rainforests. At night, the workers lock claws and form a ball, called a bivouac, to make a living nest.

◄ LIVING CUPBOARD
Honeypot ants live in dry parts of the world, including the southwest USA, Mexico and Australia. During the rainy season, the ants gather nectar. They store the sweet food in the crops (honey stomachs) of ants called repletes, whose bodies swell to form living honeypots. The repletes hang from the roof of the nest and feed the other ants during the dry season.

KEEPING COOL AND DRY ▶
Some African termites nest in tropical forests where rain falls almost every day. These species build broad caps on their ventilation chimneys to prevent rain dripping into the nest. The chimneys provide a vital cooling system. Being wingless, termites cannot keep their nests cool by fanning them with their wings, as tropical wasps and bees do.

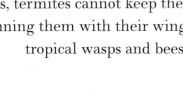

◄ TREETOP TERRITORY

These ants are gathering leaves in an African rainforest. Some tree-dwelling ants establish large treetop territories that include many nests. African weaver ant colonies, for instance, can contain up to 150 nests in 20 different trees. The ants patrol a territory of 1,600 sq metres – one of the largest insect territories ever known.

PINEFOREST HOME ►

A wasp queen perches on her home. In rainy parts of the world, wasps' nests with open cells are constructed with the cells facing downwards, so rainwater can't collect in them. Other species build an outer covering around the nest to protect the young wasps from the elements.

▲ MOUNTAIN-DWELLER

Bumblebees live mainly in northern temperate regions where the climate is coolish. In winter, the queen hibernates in a burrow where the temperature is warmer than above ground. Her thick coat helps her to keep warm. Bumblebees also live in mountainous parts of the tropics, where the height of the land keeps the air cool.

▲ HONEYBEES IN THE RAIN

Honeybees normally shelter on the comb inside the hive or nest cavity in rainy weather and do not venture outside to forage. If the comb becomes exposed to the elements for any reason, the bees will adopt a head-up position when it rains, so the water drains off their bodies

225

How Social Insects

THE QUEEN'S SCENT

Honeybee workers lick and stroke their queen to pick up her pheromones. If the queen is removed from the nest, her supply of pheromones stops. The workers rear new queens who will produce the vital scents.

Communication is the key to the smooth running of social insect colonies. Colony members interact using smell, taste, touch and sound. Social insects that can see also communicate through sight. Powerful scents called pheromones are the most important means of passing on information. These strong smells, given off by special glands, are used to send a wide range of messages that influence nestmates' behaviour. Workers release an alarm pheromone to rally their comrades to defend the colony. Ground-dwelling ants and termites smear a scent on the ground to mark the trail to food. Queens give off pheromones that tell the workers she is alive and well.

TERMITE PHEROMONES

A queen termite spends her life surrounded by workers who are attracted by her pheromones. Different scents cause her workers to fetch food, tend the young and enlarge or clean the nest.

FRIEND OR FOE?

Two black ants meet outside the nest and touch antennae to identify one another. They are checking for the particular scent given off by all colony members. Ants with the correct scent are greeted as nestmates. 'Foreign' ants will probably be attacked.

Communicate

THIS WAY, PLEASE

A honeybee worker exposes a scent gland in her abdomen to release a special scent that rallies her fellow workers. The scent from this gland, called the Nasonov gland, is used to mark sources of water. It is also used like a homing beacon to guide other bees during swarming, when the insects fly in search of a new nest.

ALARM CALL

These honeybees have come to the hive entrance to confront an enemy. When alarmed, honeybees acting as guards give off an alarm pheromone that smells like bananas. The scent tells the other bees to come to the aid of the guards against an enemy. In dangerous 'killer bee' species, the alarm pheromone prompts all hive members to attack, not just those guarding the nest.

SCENT TRAIL

This wood ant worker has captured a worm. The ant is probably strong enough to drag this small, helpless victim back to the nest herself. A worker that comes across larger prey returns to the nest to fetch her comrades, rubbing her abdomen along the ground to leave a scent trail as she does so. Her fellow workers simply follow the smelly trail to find the food. Ants can convey as many as 50 different messages by releasing pheromones and through other body language.

The Search for Food

Social insects work in teams to bring back food for the colony. Experienced workers acting as scouts forage (search) for new food sources. When they are successful, they return to the nest and communicate their information to their comrades. The workers are then able to visit the same food source. Ants mark the trail to the food with pheromones.

Bees and wasps fly back to the nest with their food. Some ants carry food to the nest in long lines, guarded by soldiers. They may need to cut up the food into manageable pieces, or work together to lift heavy loads. Worker wasps feed their young on chewed-up insects. In return, the larvae produce a sweet saliva which the adults feed on.

▲ STORING BUDS

These harvester ants live in the Sonoran Desert, western USA. They take seeds and buds back to the nest to store in special chambers called granaries. Ants that live in dry places put food aside for the times when there is nothing to eat.

▲ MAKING MEATBALLS

A wasp converts her caterpillar prey to a ball of pulp, which will be easier to carry back to the nest. Social wasps kill their insect prey by stinging them or simply chewing them to death. The wasp then finds a safe perch and cuts off hard parts such as the wings. She chews the rest of the body into a moist ball.

▲ LARGE PRIZE

This column of Central American army ants has captured a katydid, a type of grasshopper. Soldiers holds down the struggling insect while a group of workers arrives to cut it into pieces. Army ants spend most of their lives on the move, but sometimes stay in one place while the colony's newly hatched young grow up.

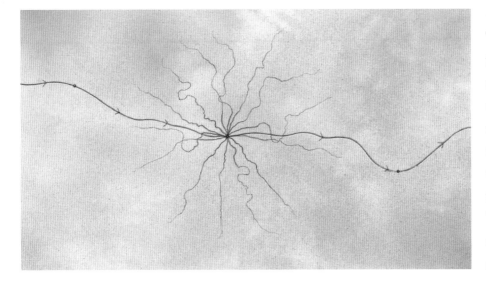

◀ **RAIDING PATTERN**
This diagram shows the temporary camp of a colony of army ants. When camping, a column of ants marches out to raid for food. Each day, the ants take a different direction, which varies about 120 degrees from the route of the previous day. Their routes form a star pattern radiating from the nest. Army ants camp for about three weeks.

▼ **AN ARMY OF TERROR**
Army ants are feared forest hunters. They mainly hunt small creatures, such as this insect, but will also kill large animals such as dogs, goats and even horses that are tied up and unable to escape.

▲ **KEPT IN THE DARK**
Termites scurry along a hidden highway they have built inside a fallen log. These insects forage widely in search of food, but seldom move into the open because bright sunlight harms them. Instead, they excavate long tunnels by digging through soft wood or earth. When moving above ground, they roof over their highways with moistened soil.

SWEET FOOD ▶
A European hornet sucks nectar from a hogweed flower. This sweet liquid forms a staple food for both adult bees and wasps. The young wasps produce a sweet saliva that the adult workers also feed on. In autumn, no more eggs are laid, so the supply of saliva stops. Deprived of this food, the wasp workers wander in search of other sweet fluids to drink, such as fruit sap.

229

Bees and Flowers

Flowering plants provide bees with nectar and pollen. In turn, many plants depend on the bees to reproduce. In order to make seeds, plants must be fertilized by pollen from the same species. This process is known as pollination. Many plants are pollinated by nectar-gathering insects such as honeybees. As the bee wanders over the flower collecting food, the pollen grains stick to her hairy body. When she visits a second flower, the grains rub off to pollinate the second plant. Plants that are fertilized in this way produce flowers with bright colours, sweet scents and special shapes to attract the insects.

Back at the nest, the pollen and nectar are fed to the other bees or stored in larder cells. The nectar is concentrated and matures to make honey. Bee scouts tell other workers about sites with many flowers by performing a special dance.

▲ **WHERE THE BEE SUCKS**
A white-tailed bumblebee approaches a foxglove, attracted by its sweet scent. The plant's bell-shaped flowers are just the right size for the bee to enter.

▲ **BUSY AS A BEE**
A white-tailed bumblebee worker feeds from a thistle. If the weather is good, a bee may visit up to 10,000 flowers in a single day.

◄ **HONEY TUMMY**
A honeybee sucks up nectar with her long tongue and stores it in her honey stomach. She may visit up to 1,000 flowers before her honey stomach is full and she returns to the nest.

GUIDING LIGHT ▶

In ultraviolet light, dark lines or markings show up on flowers such as this potentilla. Called nectar guides, the markings radiate out from the centres of flowers, which often contain nectar. The markings are very noticeable to bees, who can see ultraviolet light. They guide the insect to the flower's centre, where she can gather food.

Circular dance   Figure-of-eight dance

◀ BEE DANCES

Honeybees perform a dance to tell their nestmates where nectar-producing flowers are. When the flowers are close, the bee performs a circular dance on the comb, first in one direction, then in the other. If the food is far way, the bee performs a figure-of-eight dance, waggling her abdomen as she reaches the middle of the figure. The angle between the line of waggles and the vertical is the same as the angle between the sun, the hive and the food.

ROBBER BEE ▶

A honeybee gathers nectar from a runner bean flower. Not all bee visits help plants to reproduce. Some bees gather nectar by biting a hole in the base of the flower so the insect avoids being dusted with pollen. The bee gets her food, but far from helping the plant with pollination, she damages the flower. This process is known as robbing. This honeybee is re-using a hole made by a bumblebee.

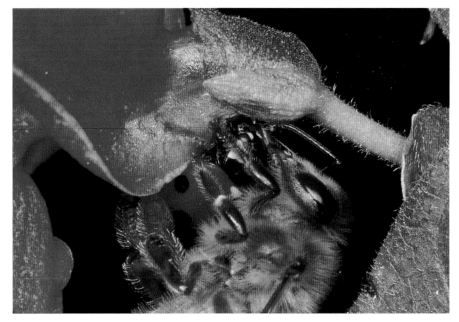

Life Cycle of Bees and Wasps

There are four different stages in the life cycle of bees and wasps. They start life as eggs, and hatch into worm-like larvae (grubs). The larvae are fed by the workers, so they do not need legs to move about and find food. When fully grown, the larva enters a resting stage and is called a pupa. Sealed inside its cell, the larva's body breaks down into mush and is reformed into an adult bee or wasp. Finally, the fully-formed adult breaks out of its cell. This process is called complete metamorphosis.

For much of the year, only sterile (non-breeding) worker wasps and bees develop. During the breeding season, male insects and young queens are reared. Some bees fly off and mate high in the air. The queens store sperm (male sex cells) in their abdomen. The males die soon after, but the young queens live on and begin to lay eggs.

▲ FROM EGG TO LARVAE
Honeybees begin life as pale, pin-sized eggs, like the ones seen here on the right. The eggs hatch and grow into fat, shiny grubs, seen here coiled in their cells. Like all bees and wasps, the queen controls the sex of the grubs. If she fertilises the egg with sperm, it develops into a female (and becomes either a queen or a worker). Unfertilised eggs develop into male drones.

▲ MATING WASPS
A male wasp courts a queen by stroking her with his antennae and rubbing his abdomen on hers. Soon the insects will mate. In temperate regions, male wasps and young queens emerge in late summer, then fly away from the nest and find mates.

HONEYBEE PUPA ▶
This pale form is a honeybee pupa. Inside, the transparent case, the insect has developed legs, wings, eyes, antennae and all the other adult body parts. The young bee will soon emerge. In honeybees, the queens, drones and workers take different amounts of time to develop. Workers take 21 days, drones take 24, while queens develop in only 16 days.

SWARM SCOUTS ▶

Bees start new colonies by swarming, as shown here. The queen leaves the nest with half her workers in a swarm (group), leaving the nest to a young, fertilized queen. The swarming bees gather in a buzzing ball on a tree branch, while scouts, in the foreground, fly off to find a new nest site. They return and perform a dance to tell the other bees where the new site is. Then the swarm flies there and builds the new nest.

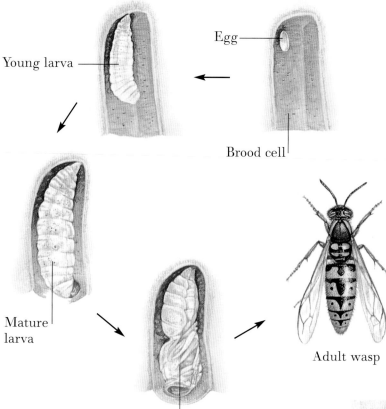

Young larva

Egg

Brood cell

Mature larva

Pupa

Adult wasp

◀ FROM EGG TO WORKER

This diagram shows the life cycle of a wasp. The queen lays a tiny egg at the bottom of each brood cell, which hatches out into a legless grub. The grub is fed by the queen or the workers on a rich diet of chewed insects, and grows quickly. When fully grown, the larva pupates to emerge as an adult wasp.

BIRTH OF A WASP ▶

A young tree wasp emerges from its brood cell, transformed from larva to adult. It breaks through the silken cap that it spun to close the cell before becoming a pupa. (Bee cells are sealed with wax by the workers.) This cell will soon be cleaned by a worker so another egg can be laid inside. Wasps take between 7 and 20 days to grow from egg to adult, depending on their species and the climate.

Young Ants and Termites

Like wasps and bees, ants have a four-stage life cycle. From eggs, they hatch into legless grubs. When they are large enough, they become pupae, and then adults.

For most of the year, the ant colony rears only sterile workers, but during the breeding season, fertile males and females appear. Unlike other ants, these have wings. During her mating flight, a queen receives a store of sperm, which will fertilize all the eggs she will lay in her lifetime.

Termites have a different life cycle with only three stages. From eggs, they hatch into young called nymphs, which look like the adults but are smaller. The nymphs feed and grow and gradually reach full size.

▲ BABYSITTING DUTY
Black ant workers tend the colony's young – the small, transparent grubs and large, pale, sausage-shaped pupae. Workers feed the grubs for a few weeks until they are ready to become pupae. Some ant larvae spin themselves a protective silk cocoon before pupating. They emerge as adults after a few weeks.

▲ MOVING THE BROOD
Weaver ant workers in an African forest have assembled the colony's eggs, grubs and pupae on a leaf before carrying them to a new site. The larvae produce silk, which the workers will use to create a new, leafy nest-ball.

UP AND AWAY ▶
A group of young black ant queens launch themselves on their mating flight. During the mating flight, the young queen may mate with one or several males. She returns to the ground to rejoin her old nest as an extra queen, or to start a new colony.

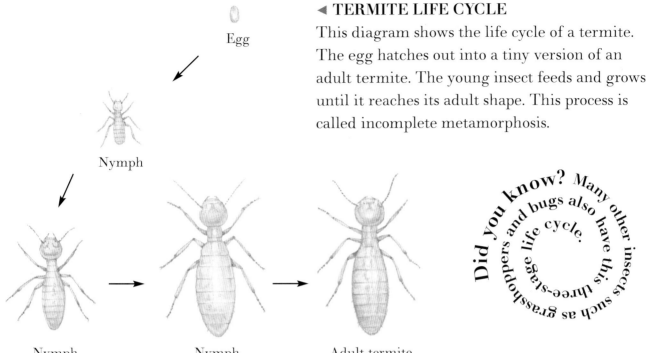

Egg

Nymph

Nymph

Nymph

Nymph

Adult termite

◄ TERMITE LIFE CYCLE

This diagram shows the life cycle of a termite. The egg hatches out into a tiny version of an adult termite. The young insect feeds and grows until it reaches its adult shape. This process is called incomplete metamorphosis.

Did you know? Many other insects such as grasshoppers and bugs also have this three-stage life cycle.

TERMITE DEVELOPMENT ►

For a long time, experts thought that termite castes were determined during reproduction, and that workers and soldiers were naturally sterile. Recently it has been discovered that the insects absorb chemicals from the queen in their food that prevent them from becoming fertile. If the king and queen die, nymphs at a particular stage in their growing cycle develop reproductive organs and become new kings or queens.

◄ FOUNDERS OF A NEW COLONY

Winged, fertile male and female termites, shown here, develop in termite colonies during the breeding season. They have harder, darker bodies than other termites, and compound eyes so they can see. These fertile insects fly off and pair up to start new colonies. They shed their wings, but the male does not die as in other types of social insects. He stays with the queen and fertilises her eggs to father all the insects in the colony.

Insect Enemies

Bees, wasps, ants and termites provide a rich source of food for many animal predators, ranging from large mammals to birds, lizards, frogs, toads and minibeasts. A bees' nest, in particular, contains a feast of different foods – stored honey and pollen, young bees and even beeswax. Bears, badgers and bee-eater birds tear into the nest to eat the contents. Some insects, such as waxmoths, are specialized to feed on particular bee products, including, as their name suggests, wax.

Bees try to defend the nest with their stings, but may not manage to fight off their enemies. Wasp, ant and termite nests contain only large numbers of young insects, but they still provide a good meal.

▲ **FOREST FEAST**
Silky anteaters live in the forests of Central and South America. They feed on forest-dwelling ants and termites. Like other mammals that eat ants, they have long snouts, sticky tongues and sharp claws.

▲ **GRASSLAND ANTEATER**
This giant anteater is probing a termite mound with its long, sticky tongue. These bushy-tailed mammals, which live in Central and South American grasslands, are major enemies of ants and termites.

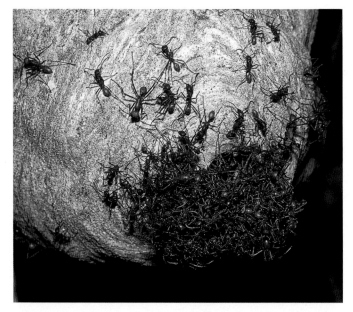

▲ **INVASION FORCE**
These army ants are invading a wasps' nest. They will break into the wasps' nest to steal – and later feast on – the young wasps. Army ants are enemies of many social insects, including other types of ants and termites.

236

◄ FOLLOW THE BIRD

This bird is a honey guide, and it is found in Africa and western Asia. Its favourite foods are found in bees' nests. It can't attack a nest by itself, so it enlists the help of a mammal called a honey badger, or ratel. The honey guide makes a special call and the badger follows the bird to the bee's nest. The ratel breaks open the nest to get to the honey, allowing the bird to feed on the bee larvae, the wax and the remains of the honey. Honey guides also lead people to bees' nests for the same reason.

BLOOD-SUCKING PARASITE ►

One of a bee colony's worst enemies is a tiny creature called the varroa mite. This photograph of the mite has been magnified many times. This eight-legged creature lives on the bee's skin and sucks its blood. Some varroa mites carry disease.

Another type of mite, the tracheal mite, infests the bee's breathing tubes. The two types of mites have destroyed thousands of bee colonies worldwide in the last ten years.

◄ EATEN ALIVE

This solitary wasp, called a bee-killer, has captured and paralyzed a worker bee and is dragging it to its burrow. There the bee will become food for the wasp's young. At the burrow, the bee-killer wasp lays an egg on the unlucky worker. When the young wasp larva hatches out, it feeds on the still-living bee.

237

Solitary Relatives

Bees, wasps, ants and termites are the only types of insects that include truly social species. However, many types of bees and wasps are solitary, and do not rear their own young.

Leafcutter bee
(*Megachile* species)

After mating, the female lays her eggs, often in a specially prepared nest stocked with food for the babies. Solitary wasps provide insect prey for their young to feed on. Solitary bees lay in a store of bee-bread, which is a mixture of nectar and pollen. Then the female flies away and takes no further care of her young.

In the wider world of insects, a few other species show some social behaviour. Female earwigs tend their eggs, and shield bugs stay with their young and guard them from enemies. However, they are not truly social because they do not work together to raise their young, or have castes that perform different tasks in the colony.

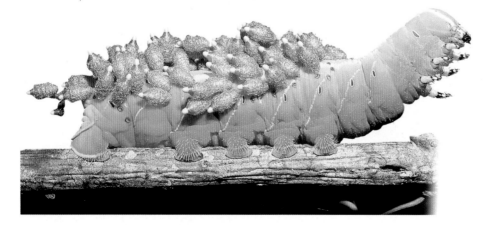

◄ **PREPARING THE NEST**
This leafcutter bee is carrying a piece of leaf to her nest. Solitary bees, such as this one, build underground nests for their young. They line the nests with pieces of leaf or petal that they snip off with their scissor-like jaws.

▲ **STOCKING UP**
This potter wasp has paralyzed a caterpillar and is dragging it back to the nest for its young to feed on when it hatches. This solitary wasp gets its name from the pot-shaped nests it moulds from clay.

◄ **PARASITIC WASPS**
Braconid wasp larvae emerge from a hawkmoth caterpillar when they are ready to pupate. This family of wasps builds no nests for their young. Instead, they lay their eggs in slow-moving insects such as caterpillars. When the eggs hatch, the larvae feast off their host as parasites.

HIBERNATING IN CLUSTERS ▶

Monarch butterflies show some signs of social behaviour. They have gathered in a flock to hibernate on a sheltered tree. In autumn, monarch butterflies fly hundreds of kilometres south to spend the winter in warmer countries. In spring, they fly north again to lay their eggs.

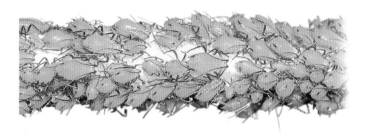

▲ GROUP FEEDERS

In summer, rose aphids gather on the stems and leaves of garden plants to suck juicy plant sap. The insects may collect together on their favourite food plants, but do not actively cooperate with one another, and so are not classed as social.

Field digger wasp
(*Mellinus arvensis*)

◀ TAKEAWAY SUPPER

This field digger wasp is carrying a captured fly to her underground burrow, where it will feed her young. Instead of stinging their victims, some types of solitary wasps bite their prey to kill or subdue them, before using them to stock their nests.

Did you know? Some solitary mason bees build clay nests on walls, or lay their eggs in abandoned snail shells.

INSECT SWARMS ▶

Locusts are relatives of grasshoppers and live mostly in hot, dry countries. During the long, dry season, locusts are solitary, but when rain falls and plants bloom, they gather and breed quickly to form large swarms. The adult locusts gather in huge, destructive swarms and fly around the countryside looking for food.

How Insects Evolved

Insects are a very ancient group of creatures. They started to evolve from common ancestors about 400 million years ago and developed into about 30 or so orders (types). Insects were the first creatures to fly and some evolved wings more than 350 million years ago.

Relatively few fossils of prehistoric insects survive because insects are so small and fragile. However, some fossils have been preserved in amber (hardened tree resin). Experts believe that modern ants, wasps and bees all evolved from the same wasp-like, meat-eating ancestors.

▲ FOSSILIZED IN AMBER
This prehistoric bee has been preserved in amber. About 40–50 million years ago, the bee landed on the trunk of a pine tree and became trapped in the sticky resin. Later, the resin slowly hardened to become clear, golden-coloured amber, which is often used to make jewellery.

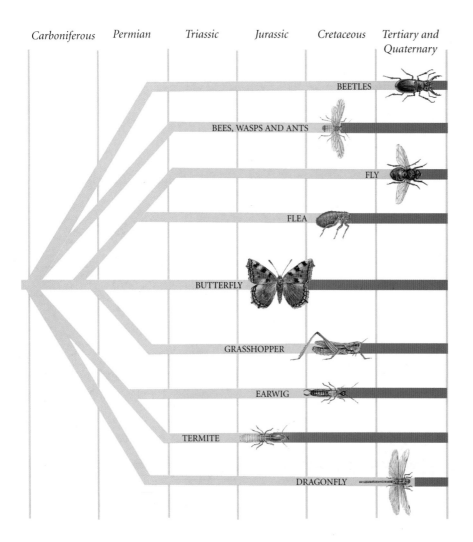

◄ INSECT EVOLUTION
This diagram shows the time period when some insect species evolved and how they are related to each other. There are more than a million different insect species divided into about 30 orders. Bees, wasps and ants belong to the order Hymenoptera. Termites belong to a separate order, Isoptera. As this diagram shows, termites developed earlier than many other insects. They are more closely related to earwigs than they are to bees, wasps and ants.

◀ ANCIENT TERMITE

This winged male termite became trapped in tree resin about 30 million years ago. As you can see, the insect's delicate wings, legs and even its antennae have been preserved in the amber. The oldest amber fossils date back to about 100 million years ago, but termites are thought to have evolved long before that.

A NEW PARTNERSHIP ▶

The ancestors of bees and wasps were meat-eaters. About 100 million years ago, bees began to feed on pollen and nectar from newly evolved flowers. Experts think that plants developed the flowers to lure insects into helping them with pollination. The partnership between insects and flowering plants flourished and the number of both species increased greatly.

Brown bumblebee
(*Bombus pascuorum*)

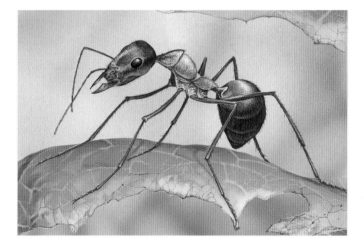

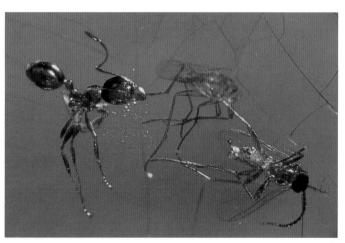

▲ TERROR OF THE PAST

About 45 million years ago, giant ants roamed the forests of Europe. This picture shows how a worker may have looked. The ants probably lived in large colonies and were carnivorous, just like many ants today. The queens were the largest ants ever to have lived and had a wing-span of up to 13cm, which is larger than some hummingbirds.

▲ PREHISTORIC HUNTER

This amber fossil contains an ant with two mosquito-like insects. The ant, a meat-eating hunter, became trapped in the resin while preying on one of the mosquitoes. Its leg can still be seen between the ant's jaws. Experts believe ants were originally ground-dwelling insects. Later they became social and began to live in underground nests.

241

Insect Societies and People

Social insects affect our lives and the world we live in. We think of some species as friends, others as enemies. Bees are important because they pollinate crops and wild plants. They also give us honey and many other products. We fear bees and wasps for their stings, which can kill if the victim has a strong allergic reaction. However, bee venom contains chemicals that are used in medicine. Wasps help us by killing huge numbers of pests that feed on farmers' crops.

Plant-eating ants damage gardens and orchards, and can spoil food stores. Some types of ants protect aphids, which are a pest in gardens, but other ants hunt and kill crop-harming pests. In tropical countries, termites cause great damage in plantations and orchards and to wooden houses. However, even termites play an important role in the cycle of life in their natural habitats.

▲ WONDERFUL WAX

Bees do not just give us honey – they also produce beeswax, which is used to make polish and candles, like the ones shown here. People eat pollen pellets collected by bees, and royal jelly, which young bees feed on, because they are healthy and nourishing.

◄ WASP SAVES CABBAGE

This hornet is eating a cabbage white caterpillar, which feeds on cabbage plants and is a pest for farmers and gardeners. Hornets are among the many wasp species that help farmers and gardeners by killing large numbers of insects that harm crops and prize plants. Other solitary species of wasps specialize in preying on aphids, caterpillars and other pests.

Did you know? In Australia, Aboriginals eat honeypot ants like sweets.

Hornet
(*Vespa crabro*)

242

▲ PLANTATION PEST

In warm countries, leafcutter ants can become a major pest in plantations and orchards. These insects need large quantities of leaves to feed the fungi in their fungus gardens. A large colony of leafcutters can strip a fruit tree bare of leaves in a single night.

▲ PROTECTING THE TREES

These weaver ants are being used to control pests in an orange orchard. In China, weaver ant nests have been sold for the last 2,000 years, making them the earliest-known form of natural pest control. Farmers hang the nests in their trees and the ants eat the harmful pests.

◄ EATING SOCIAL INSECTS

This man from West Africa is eating a fat, juicy termite queen, which is considered to be a delicacy in that part of the world. Social insects, including adult termites and young wasps, bees and ants, are eaten in many parts of the world, including Australia. In Western countries, people are squeamish about eating insects, but in some developing countries, tasty and nourishing insects provide up to 10 per cent of the animal protein in people's diets.

READ ALL ABOUT TERMITE DAMAGE ►

Wood-eating termites have damaged this book. Termites also cause major damage to timber structures in some parts of the world. Some species burrow under buildings where they damage the wooden foundations. People often do not even know the termites are there until the damage is done and the wood is eaten away. Termites also cause havoc by eating wooden sleepers used on railway tracks.

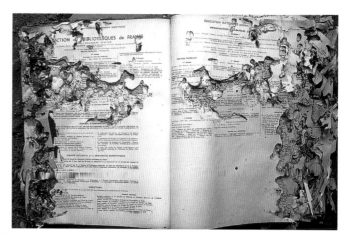

Collecting Honey

TRADITIONAL HIVES

This photo, taken around 1900, shows traditional methods of beekeeping. In past centuries, honeybees were kept in straw containers called skeps, shown here. This brave beekeeper has no protective clothing for her arms and head.

People have eaten honey as a natural delicacy since the beginning of human history. Long before written records existed, people raided wild bees' nests to harvest this sweet food. A prehistoric cave painting dating to 7000BC shows a person taking honeycomb from a bees' nest. About 3,000 years ago, people began to domesticate bees and keep them in hives so they could harvest the honey more easily. Beekeeping is now practised throughout the world.

Several different species of honeybee exist; the best known is the European honeybee which produces large amounts of honey. This bee, originally from the Middle East and Asia, was spread to Europe by travellers long ago, and later taken to North America by early settlers. Now it is found on every continent except Antarctica.

A MODERN HOME

Today, most beehives are wooden boxes containing several frames that can be removed, allowing beekeepers to reach the bees and honey. The queen and her brood live in the lower frames. The workers store nectar and pollen in the upper frames, called supers. The beekeeper harvests honey from the supers. A metal screen prevents the queen from laying eggs in the supers.

from Bees

THE BUSINESS OF POLLINATION

This field of sunflowers has been pollinated by bees. In North America and Australia, beekeeping is big business. Farmers and orchard owners hire the bees to pollinate their crops. Beekeepers travel thousands of kilometres to move their bees to regions where plants are flowering and producing nectar. Many beekeeping businesses are run by local farmers. Others are owned by large corporations.

DIFFICULT ACCESS

In the mountain kingdom of Nepal in Asia, giant Himalayan honeybees nest in caves and cracks in vertical cliff faces. These bees are adapted to survive in the cold mountain climate. Local people risk their lives to reach the honey.

COVERING UP

Modern beekeepers wear protective clothing. Nylon overalls, gloves, thick boots and a hat with a veil help protect the wearer from stings. Keepers may also pacify their bees with smoke, but they still get stung frequently.

Conservation

Just as social insects affect our lives, so we affect the lives of social insects. As human populations expand, we change the wild places where insects live. For example, large areas of tropical rainforest are being felled for timber or fuel, and to build settlements. This threatens the survival of the forest's plants and animals, including social insects. In developed countries all over the world, farms cover large areas that used to be wild. Crops are a feast for some insect pests, so their numbers multiply quickly. Many farmers use chemical insecticides to protect their crops from the pests, but these chemicals kill 'helpful' insects along with the pests.

All over the world, conservationists fight to save rare animal species, such as tigers. It is important that we start to protect social insects, too.

▲ POISON SPRAY
A tractor sprays insecticide over a field. The poisonous chemicals kill not only pests but also other insects such as bees, which pollinate flowers, and wasps, which prey on the pests. Some types of insecticide are now banned because they damage and pollute the natural world. Herbicides designed to control weeds also kill wild plants that social insects feed on.

◄ FOREST DESTRUCTION
A forest is being felled for timber. The tropical rainforests contain over half of all known animal species, including thousands of social insects. Destroying forests affects not only large animals but also tiny insects. Experts fear that some social insects in these huge forests may become extinct before they have even been identified.

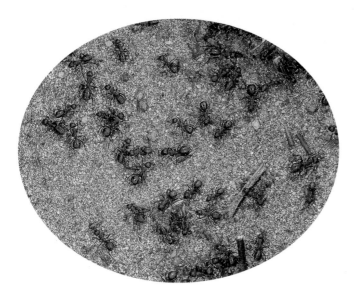

◀ PROTECTED BY LAW

In temperate forests, wood ant colonies do a vital job in preying on insects that harm the forest. In Aachen, Germany, in 1880, the wood ant became the first insect to be protected by a conservation law. It is now protected in several other European countries. Foresters also help to protect the insects by screening off their mounds to prevent people from stealing the young ants to use as fish food. Although one wood ants' nest may contain up to a million insects, including several hundred queens, it is still vulnerable to human destruction.

HELPING THE FOREST ▶

Termites become our enemies when they move into our houses and eat wooden beams and furniture. People kill them using poisonous chemicals. In the wild, however, even these unpopular insects do a useful job. As they munch through leaves and wood, they help to break down plant matter so the goodness it contains returns to fertilize the soil.

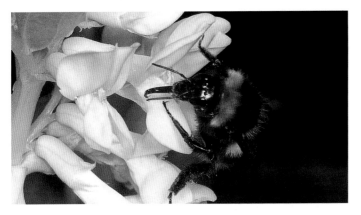

◀ RARE BEE

A long-tongued bumblebee feeds from a field bean flower. This and several other crops can only be pollinated by bumblebees with long tongues. In some areas, however, domestic honeybees now thrive at the expense of the native long-tongued bees. When the long-tongued bees become scarce, the plants that depend on them for pollination are threatened too.

VITAL FOR POLLINATION ▶

Many of our most popular fruits, vegetables and other crops are pollinated by honeybees. These include apples, pears, melons, onions, carrots, turnips and cotton. Experts estimate that up to a third of all human foods depend on bees for pollination.

GLOSSARY

abdomen
The rear part of an insect's body. This section contains the reproductive organs and part of the digestive system.

adapt
When an animal, or group of animals, changes in order to survive in new conditions.

amber
A type of fossilized tree resin, which is often used to make jewellery.

ambush
To hide and wait, and then make a surprise attack.

androconia
Androconia are the special scales on a male butterfly's wings that release scent to attract female butterflies.

antenna
The plural of antenna is antennae. Antennae are the two long projections or 'feelers' on top of an insect's head, which it uses to smell, touch and taste. These feelers are the insect's most important sense receptors. Some antennae may even pick up taste and changes in temperature.

arachnid
Member of a group of small meat-eating animals with simple eyes and eight legs. They include spiders, mites, ticks and scorpions.

araneidae
The family of spiders that usually build orb webs.

araneomorph
A typical or true spider with jaws that can close together sideways.

arthropod
An animal without a backbone that has many jointed legs and an exoskeleton on the outside of its body. Arthropods include spiders, insects, crabs and woodlice.

ballooning
When spiders float away on strands of silk blown by the wind.

basal region
The basal region is the part of a butterfly's wing that lies closest to its body.

book lung
An organ in a spider's body that takes oxygen from the air. Most spiders have one pair of book lungs found in the abdomen with an air-filled cavity filled with layers (like the pages of a book). The blood that flows through the layers takes in oxygen.

brood cells
The cells inside a bees' or wasps' nest in which the young insects grow and develop.

camouflage
The colours and patterns on an animal's body that blend in with its surroundings. Thishelps an animal to hide from its enemies or creep up on its prey.

carapace
The shell-like covering over the front part of a spider's body, the cephalothorax.

carnivore
An animal that feeds on the flesh of other animals.

carrion
Remains of a dead animal.

caste
A particular type of insect within a colony, which performs certain special tasks.

caterpillar
The second or 'larval' stage in the life of a butterfly or moth, after it has hatched. A caterpillar has a long tube-like body with 13 segments, powerful biting jaws and many legs. It has no wings and may be brightly coloured, hairy or spiny.

cells
(1) The six-sided containers inside a bees' or wasps' nest, in which the young insects grow and where bees store their food. (2) Any area of a butterfly's wing that is enclosed by veins – but especially the oval cell near the middle of the wing, which is called the discal cell.

cephalothorax
The front part of a spider's body, to which the legs are attached.

chelicerae
The jaws of a spider.

chrysalis
The third or 'pupal' stage of many butterflies' lives, when they transform into adults, often inside hard, bean-shaped shells.

classification
Arranging animals according to their similarities and differences in order to study them and suggest how they may be related.

cocoon
(1) A bag or shelter spun from silk thread by some caterpillars, especially those of moths, in which they pupate into an adult. (2) A silky covering or egg case made to protect a spider's eggs. (3) Another term for a pupa.

colony
A large group of insects that live together.

comb
The flat sheets inside a bees' or wasps' nest made up of hundreds of cells joined together.

compound eyes
The large eyes found on wasps, bees, butterflies, moths and other insects, which are made up of many different lenses.

crab spiders
Ambushing spiders in the family Thomisidae that do not usually build webs and are often shaped rather like crabs.

cribellum
A plate through which a special kind of fine, woolly silk is produced in a group of spiders known as the cribellates (lace-web weavers). The plate is just in front of the spinnerets at the back of the abdomen.

crop
A part of the digestive system that some insects use to store food. In honey bees this is known as the honey stomach.

cuticle
The tough substance that forms the outer skin of an insect.

daddy-longlegs spiders
Spiders in the family Pholcidae. They have very long legs and build untidy webs under stones, in caves or the corners of rooms.

diet
The range of food and drink that an animal eats.

digestion
The process by which food is broken down so it can be taken into the body.

discal cell
see cell (2).

dragline
The line of silk on which a spider drops down, often to escape from danger, and then climbs back up.

drone
A male bee.

ecdysis
When caterpillars moult (shed their skin) as they grow, the process is known as ecdysis.

elytra (singular: elytron)
The hardened wing cases of a beetle that have evolved from the insect's front wings. When the beetle is on the ground, the elytra fold over and protect its delicate back wings.

embolus
A structure at the end of a male spider's palp that is used to transfer sperm to the female.

evolve
An animal species is said to evolve when it changes gradually, over many generations, thus becoming better suited to the particular conditions in which it lives.

exoskeleton
The hard outer skin of an insect that protects the soft parts inside.

extinct
An animal or plant species is said to be extinct when it dies out completely.

family
A scientific classification grouping together related animals or plants. Families are sub-divided into genera.

fang
The piercing part of a spider's jaw. Poison comes out of a hole at the tip of the fang.

fertile
An animal that is able to produce young after mating. In social insects, the only fertile female is the queen.

fertilization
The joining together of a male sperm and a female egg to start a new life.

food plant
Any particular plant on which a caterpillar or other insect is known to feed.

fossil
The preserved remains of an animal or its prints, which are often found in rock but are also found in amber.

frenulum
The hook-like bristles that hold the forewing of a moth to its hindwing.

genus (plural: genera)
A scientific classification grouping together related animals or plants. Genera are sub-divided into species.

gill
Part of an animal's body, which it uses to help it breathe under water. An insect's gills are often feathery.

gland
An organ in an animal's body that produces a substance, often a liquid, that has a particular use. Spiders have silk glands for spinning silk and poison glands linked to fangs for making and storing poison.

grub
The legless larva of an insect such as a wasp or bee.

habitat
The particular place in which an animal species lives, such as a rainforest or a desert.

halteres
The balancing organs of flies. Halteres are the remnants of the hind wings and look like tiny drumsticks.

hibernation
A time when an insect is inactive or sleeping during the cold, winter months.

honeydew
A sweet fluid given off by such sap-sucking insects such as aphids, and eaten by some types of ants.

honey stomach
The organ in a honeybee's body where nectar is stored. It is also known as the crop.

hub
The central circle of an orb web made by a spider.

insect
A small animal with a body that is divided into three parts, with six legs and usually one or two pairs of wings.

imago
The scientific name for the adult stage in the life of a moth or butterfly, when it has wings.

insect
One of a group of invertebrate animals (ones with no backbone). An insect has three body parts – head, thorax and abdomen.

instar
A stage in the life of a butterfly or moth between any two moults or dramatic changes. The first instar is the newly hatched caterpillar. After its first moult, it enters the second instar. The final instar is the adult stage.

invertebrate
An animal without an internal skeleton. Insects with an exoskeleton, are invertebrates.

jumping spiders
Spiders in the family Salticidae that are curious, daytime hunters with two stout front pairs of legs.

king
The fertile male termite who fertilizes the queen's eggs.

larva
The plural of larva is larvae. The young of insects that undergo complete metamorphosis, such as beetles, butterflies and true flies.

leaf litter
The top layer of a forest floor, consisting of dead and decomposing leaves.

leaf mining
Describes how small caterpillars eat tunnels through the insides of leaves.

lens
Part of an animal's eye, which helps it to see.

Lepidoptera
The scientific name for the group of insects made up of butterflies and moths. Lepidoptera comes from Ancient Greek and means 'scaly wings'.

life cycle
A series of stages in the lives of animals such as insects, as they grow up and become adults. There are four stages in a beetle's life cycle – first as an egg, then as a larva or grub, as a pupa and as an adult. A bug passes through three stages in its life cycle – as an egg, a nymph and an adult. There are four stages in the life cycles of butterflies and moths – egg, caterpillar or larva, pupa and adult butterfly or moth.

lynx spiders
Spiders in the family Oxopidae that hunt on plants. They have pointed abdomens, spiny legs and fairly large eyes. Females fix their egg cases to plants and guard them until they hatch.

lyriform organs
Sensory organs, especially on a spider's legs, that sense vibrations when an insect is trapped in a web.

malpighian tubes
Tubes leading into the junction of an insect's mid and hind gut, involved in urine formation.

mammal
A warm-blooded animal with a bony skeleton. Mammals feed their young on milk.

mandibles
A pair of jaws at the sides of an insect's mouth, which are used for biting, crushing and cutting food.

mating
When a male and female animal come together to produce young.

maxillae
The pair of weaker, lower mouthparts or jaws of an insect. Spiders use these to turn prey into a liquid pulp.

membrane
A thin skin.

metamorphosis
The transformation of a young insect into an adult. Bees, ants and wasps have a four-stage life cycle – egg, larva, pupa and adult. They are said to exhibit complete metamorphosis. Termites have a three-stage cycle – egg, nymph and adult. They are said to exhibit incomplete metamorphosis. Beetles have four stages in their life cycle: egg, larva, pupa and adult. This is called complete metamorphosis. Bugs have only three stages in their life cycle: egg, nymph and adult. They undergo incomplete metamorphosis.

migration
The regular journeys made by butterflies and moths to follow seasonal changes in the weather. Butterflies are unlike birds in that most migrate one way and do not return to their original homes.

mimicry
When a spider or other insect copies the shape of another animal or an object such as a bird dropping or stick. Spiders use mimicry to hide from their enemies and prey.

minibeasts
Insects and similar small animals such as spiders, woodlice, scorpions and centipedes.

moult
When a young, growing insect sheds its skin and grows a new, larger one, inside which there is room for it to grow.

mygalomorph
A primitive spider with jaws that strike downward. They have two pairs of book lungs and no tracheae. Most species are large, hairy and live in burrows, such as trapdoor spiders and tarantulas.

nectar
A sweet liquid found in flowers is eaten by insects such as wasps and bees. Plants produce nectar to encourage insects to visit the flower and pollinate it.

nocturnal
An animal that rests by day and is active during the night. Many moths are nocturnal.

nursery-web spiders
Pisauridae spiders who carry egg cases in their jaws.

nymph
The young of insects which undergo incomplete metamorphis, such as bugs, grasshoppers and dragonflies. Newly hatched bugs are called nymphs and look like tiny adults, but they are wingless.

order
A scientific category, such as insects, describing a group of animals with a range of shared characteristics.

ovipositor
The tube through which a female butterfly or moth pushes her eggs on to a leaf.

palps
Short feelers on an insect's mouth that help it to find and guide food into the mouth. They act as sense detectors and play an important part in finding food and food plants.

paralyse
To make an animal powerless and unable to move, although it is still alive.

parasite
An animal that lives on or inside another animal and lives off it, sometimes killing it.

parthenogenesis
The process by which some female insects can reproduce without mating.

pheromones
Special scents given off by animals, such as insects, at certain times to communicate with others of their species, especially to mate.

pollen
The dust-like yellow powder produced by plants. Bees use pollen, together with honey or nectar, to feed their larvae. When they collect pollen, bees fertilize flowers in a process called pollination.

pollination
The transfer of pollen from the male part of a flower to the female part, so that the plant can be fertilized and produce seeds.

predator
An animal that hunts and eats other animals for food.

prey
An animal that is hunted and eaten by a predator.

proboscis
The long, thin tongue of a butterfly or moth. It is used to suck up nectar from flowers.

propolis
A sticky tree resin used by worker honeybees to repair cracks in their nest. It is also known as 'bee glue'.

puddling
When a butterfly or moth drinks from a muddy pool or puddle.

pupa
The plural of pupa is pupae. The third stage in the lives of insects such as wasps, ants and bees before they become adults. This is the third major stage in the life of a butterfly or moth, when it changes from a caterpillar to an adult – often inside a cocoon.

pupation
The change from caterpillar to pupa or chrysalis.

queen
A fertile female insect within a social insect colony, whose job is to lay eggs. In social insects, the only fertile female is the queen.

recluse spiders
Spiders in the family Loxoscelidae that are very poisonous to people and often spin webs in buildings.

retinaculum
The catch that holds the frenulum. It is used to hook together the forewing and hindwing of a moth.

roosting
Sleeping in a safe place.

rostrum
The long snout of a weevil. The beetle's jaws, and sometimes its eyes, are found at the tip of the long snout. The antennae are often positioned halfway down the beetle's rostrum.

scales
The small, thin plates that cover the wing of a butterfly or moth.

scavenger
An animal that feeds on rubbish, recycling waste by consuming dead plants and the remains of animals or eating food humans do not consider edible, such as clothes, woollen carpets, wooden furniture or animal dung.

scopula
A dense brush of hairs on the feet of some spiders that helps them to grip smooth surfaces.

simple eyes
The small, bead-like eyes possessed by insects such as wasps, which can detect the level of light.

social
Living with others of its species in a co-operative group. The colonies of social insects contain different castes and at least two generations. All the insects help to rear the colony's young.

soldier
A caste of insects within a social insect colony, who defend their nestmates and the nest.

species
A group of animals or plants that share similar characteristics and can breed together to produce fertile young..

sphragis
The horny pouch that male Apollo butterflies ooze on to a female to prevent her mating again.

spiderling
A young spider that looks more or less like the fully-grown adult.

spinneret
(1) The organ of a caterpillar through which silk emerges.
(2) An opening at the end of a spider's abdomen through which silk is pulled out.

spiracles
The tiny holes in an insect's exoskeleton, through which air passes into breathing tubes, allowing it to breathe.

spitting spiders
Spiders in the family Scytodidae with a domed carapace and large venom glands that produce glue as well as venom.

stabilimentum
A band of white silk, placed across the centre of some spiders' webs.

stridulate
When an insect produces sound by rubbing parts of the body together.

succinct pupa
A pupa or chrysalis that is held pointing up by a silken thread.

suspended pupa
The pupa or chrysalis of a butterfly or moth, which hangs down from a small pad of silk.

tarantula
One of the giant, hairy spiders belonging to the family Theraphosidae. In Australia, it is often the name given to the huntsman spiders. The true tarantula is a wolf spider from the genus *Lycosa* found in southern Europe.

tarsi
The feet of a butterfly or moth. The tarsi often contain important taste organs.

territory
An area that an animal uses for feeding or breeding. Animals will defend their territory against others of its species.

thorax
The middle part of the three body sections of an insect to which the wings and legs are attached. The thorax is packed with strong muscles that move the wings and legs.

trachea
The plural of trachea is tracheae. Fine tubes through which air is carried around the spider's body. They open to the outside through holes called spiracles.

trichobothrium
The plural of trichobothrium is trichobothria. It is a long, fine hair on a spider's leg that detects air vibrations. Sometimes called a touch-at-a-distance receptor.

tympanal organs
The 'ears' on the abdomen or thorax of an insect.

uloboridae
Feather-legged spiders that are the only spiders without venom.

veins
The thin, hollow tubes which support an insect's wings. Veins are the supporting framework of the wing of a butterfly or moth. The pattern of veins is often used to classify butterflies and moths.

venom
Poisonous fluid produced by nearly all spiders that is used to kill their prey.

warning colours
Distinctive colours, often combinations of red, yellow and black, which are common to many foul-tasting or poisonous animals, and which warn predators away.

wolf spiders
Members of the family Lycosidae.

worker
The non-breeding insects in a social insect colony who perform many tasks for the group.

253

INDEX

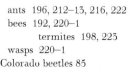

Conservation Addresses

About
http://insects.about.com

Born Free Foundation (UK)
http://www.bornfree.org.uk
3 Grove House, Foundry Lane, Horsham
West Sussex, RH13 5PL UK
tel: 01403 240170

British Butterfly Conservation Society Ltd
Manor Yard. East Lulworth, near Wareham
Dorset BH20 5QP UK
    http://www.butterfly-conservation.org
        tel. 01929 400209

**Children's International Wildlife
    Sanctuary (USA)**
    http://www.ciws.org
    P.O. Box 379, Saratoga
    NY 12866-0379 USA

Ecobeetle
    http://www.ecobeetle.com

Greenpeace International
    http://www.greenpeace.org
    Keizersgracht 176, 1016 DW Amsterdam
    The Netherlands
    tel: 31 20 523 62 22

North American Butterfly Association (NABA)
4 Delaware Road
Morristown, NJ 07960 USA
http://www.naba.org

Wildlife Conservation Society (USA)
http://www.wcs.org
64th Street and 5th Avenue, New York, USA
tel: (718) 220-5111

World Wildlife Fund (WWF International)
http://www.wwf.org
Also WWF organisations in many countries including:
Australia, Austria, Belgium, Brazil, Canada, Denmark,
Finland, France, Germany, Greece, Hong Kong, India,
Indonesia, Italy, Japan, Malaysia, the Netherlands,
New Zealand, Norway, Pakistan, Philippines, Spain,
Sweden, Switzerland, the United Kingdom and the
United States of America.

WWF-UK
Panda House, Weyside Park, Godalming,
Surrey GU7 1XR UK
tel: 01483 426 444

WWF-USA
1250 24th Street, NW., P.O. Box 97180,
Washington DC 20077-7180 USA
tel: 1-800-CALL-WWF